1764

Journal of the American Revolution Books highlight the latest research on new or lesser-known topics of the revolutionary era. The *Journal of the American Revolution* is an online resource and annual volume that provides educational, peer-reviewed articles by professional historians and experts in American Revolution studies.

A JOURNAL OF THE AMERICAN REVOLUTION BOOK

1764

THE FIRST YEAR
OF THE
AMERICAN REVOLUTION

KEN SHUMATE

WESTHOLME
Yardley

Westholme Publishing, LLC
904 Edgewood Road
Yardley, Pennsylvania 19067
Visit our Web site at www.westholmepublishing.com

ISBN: 978-1-59416-359-3
Also available as an eBook.

Printed in the United States of America.

CONTENTS

Contents

PREFACE

THE YEAR 1764 IS OF EXTRAORDINARY IMPORTANCE TO THE HISTORY of the American Revolution. It was a before-and-after sort of year, a tumultuous year, a watershed in the relationship between Great Britain and its colonies.

In 1763, the British began to strictly enforce the laws of trade in order to advance a newly formulated colonial policy that included use of customs duties as a means of raising revenue from the colonies. In reaction, Americans early in 1764 protested that the laws being enforced were economically unsound and would be destructive to the trade of the colonies.

Despite knowing of the American discontent, British officials moved forward with their new colonial policy, enacting a statute to levy customs duties for the purpose of revenue. British statesman Edmund Burke had it right in this observation to the House of Commons in 1774. "No act avowedly for the purpose of revenue" is found in the statute book until 1764. "All before this period stood on commercial regulation and restraint." It is the Sugar Act, he asserts, that

> opened a new principle: and here properly began the second period of the policy of this country with regard to the colonies; by which the scheme of a regular plantation parliamentary revenue

was adopted in theory, and settled in practice. A revenue not substituted in the place of, but superadded to a monopoly.[1]

At the same time as passage of the Sugar Act, the House of Commons took an even more provocative action: a resolution in March 1764 to further establish a parliamentary revenue.

Towards further defraying the said Expences, it may be proper to charge certain Stamp Duties in the said Colonies and Plantations.[2]

Burke addressed the American protests in response.

After the resolution of the House, and before the passing of the Stamp Act, the Colonies of Massachusetts Bay and New York did send remonstrances, objecting to this mode of parliamentary taxation.[3]

He went on to mention the similar petitions of Connecticut, Rhode Island, and Virginia, stressing that the protests had no effect on British decisions. At the heart of the American response in late 1764 was an examination of the constitutional relationship between the colonies and Great Britain. That examination, including a wholesale rethinking of the relationship, addressed the central issues of what would eventually become known as the Stamp Act Crisis.

The point of this book—and its focus on 1764—is to describe the actions taken by the British government, and the American reaction that prompted the sequence of events ending in American independence.

INTRODUCTION

"What do We mean by the American Revolution? Do We mean the American War? The Revolution was effected before the War commenced. The Revolution was in the Minds and Hearts of the People."

—John Adams, 1818

THE YEAR 1764 MARKED THE BEGINNING OF A LONG AND UNHAPPY argument between America and Great Britain; it was the first year of the American Revolution. The British government began to implement a change in colonial policy, from a focus on the regulation of trade to raising revenue from the colonies based on parliamentary taxation. The decisions were made in 1763, with implementation beginning in 1764. The Americans protested. My intent is to tell you the story of the change in policy and the resulting protests.

THE CHANGE IN POLICY

The British ministry took two actions in 1764. The most dramatic was the announcement of a plan to implement stamp duties as a means of imposing taxes on the colonies; this was an innovation, a tax with no constitutional precedent. The other action was the passage of the Sugar Act, intended to extract revenue from America through the use of customs duties applied to imported products. Although not at first recognized as such, this use of duties imposed for the purpose of revenue was as equally unconstitutional as was the levy of stamp duties.[1]

Benjamin Franklin was among the first to note the resulting change in the American attitude toward Great Britain. Giving testimony in the House of Commons in early 1766, he was asked, "What was the temper of America towards Great Britain before the year 1763?" He answered, "The best in the world. They submitted willingly to the government of the crown, and paid, in all their courts, obedience to acts of parliament." In phrases later famous in describing the Anglo-American relationship, he went on that "they were governed by this country at the expence only of a little pen, ink, and paper. They were led by a thread." But afterward, not so much good feeling. He was asked, "And what is their temper now?" His response: "O, very much altered."[2]

THE AMERICAN PROTESTS

There are two significant aspects to the protests of the Americans in 1764, corresponding to the two British actions. The first, in protest against the planned stamp duties, is that the colonists were not represented in Parliament, and such taxation was therefore a violation of the rights of Englishmen, a violation of the constitutional right to be taxed only with their own consent or the consent of those who represent them. Prompting this opposition, and the related "examination of the constitutional relationship between England and America," was Prime Minister George Grenville's introduction of stamp duties, "from the time he first broached the subject in the House of Commons in March 1764."[3] One outcome of the examination was that Americans made the constitutional case against taxation by Parliament in 1764, before passage of the Stamp Act in 1765.

The other significant aspect of the American protests has to do with the duties imposed by the Sugar Act. With few exceptions, the Americans did not raise a constitutional grievance about those duties but rather limited their objections to the economic burden. The lack of constitutionally based protest led British leaders to believe that save for the economic problems of high duties, the Americans had no objection to taxes levied as customs duties.[4]

William Beckford, one of America's steady allies in the opposition to taxation, made a statement in the House of Commons in February 1765 that illustrates the British understanding of the American position. He supported the right "of taxing the imports and exports of the colonies" and—the most important point for us to hear—that "the colonies all admit this principle." But he warned his colleagues that such acceptance would not extend to stamp duties. "The North Americans do not think an internal and external duty the same."[5]

In 1764, as part of a reevaluation of their relationship with the mother country, the colonies put forth constitutional arguments against taxation that would guide American response to British actions for the next decade. Understanding what went on in 1764—how the Americans responded to the new British policy—provides insight into the angry dialogue of 1765 and the eventual resistance to all parliamentary taxation.

PRESENTATION OF THE MATERIAL

My approach in presenting this material is, as much as makes sense, to allow American voices to be heard, to convey their ideas in the original eighteenth-century style and language (often including awkward spelling, punctuation, and capitalization). This approach allows you to not only understand the contents of each petition, essay, letter, or other writing but also listen to how the author made his argument. I extract and condense from the original writings in order to provide the gist of each document—and, by allowing the Americans to speak for themselves, to provide the essence as well.

I present extracts from nine colonial protests against the stamp duties, and—intertwined with the protests—extracts from each of five essays of 1764 that examine the relationship between the colonies and Great Britain. James Otis, Oxenbridge Thacher, Richard Bland, Thomas Fitch, and Stephen Hopkins wrote tracts significant in 1764 and famous today.[6]

In order to introduce these protests and essays, and enough other material to establish context, I often provide only a small part of a lengthy document. In addition, in order to tell a story of reasonable length while letting the participants speak, I restrict coverage to those events that best explain the beginning of the revolution. Although

there were many aspects to that beginning, the heart of the controversy with Great Britain in 1764 was taxation.[7] The American writings are the most illuminating expression of that controversy, and
they begin examination of the constitutional relationship between
the colonial legislatures and Parliament.[8]

As I weave together British action with American response, my
plan is to tell a story about 1764. I think it is a rousing good tale,
and I hope you enjoy it.

PROLOGUE

I N THE EARLY EIGHTEENTH CENTURY, THE ECONOMY OF THE BRITISH colonies in North America was dependent on imported molasses, there distilled into rum for domestic consumption and—of particular importance—as an export necessary to obtain specie required for the purchase of British manufactured goods. The Americans imported molasses from sugar islands in the West Indies, most often in exchange for fish, beef, lumber, horses, and other provisions necessary for the livelihood of the largely single-crop plantations. Plantation owners in the British sugar islands, in dire competition with the French and Dutch, resented that their sibling colonies provided the foreign sugar islands with these indispensable supplies and complained to British officials that the trade should be prohibited. The Americans maintained that the trade was necessary since the British islands could not provide sufficient molasses to meet American needs; nor could the British islands take all the produce needed to be exported from the northern colonies.[1]

Eventually, the British sugar planters persuaded the House of Commons to stop the trade between the Americans and the foreign colonies. The method of ending the trade was not outright prohibition but the levy of high customs duties on imports from the foreign colonies. The resulting statute was the Sugar Act of 1733 (6 George II c. 13).[2]

The title.

An act for the better *securing and encouraging the trade* of his
Majesty's sugar colonies in America.

The preamble.

Whereas the welfare and prosperity of your Majesty's sugar
colonies in America are of the greatest consequence and importance to the trade, navigation, and strength of this kingdom; and
whereas the planters of the said sugar colonies have of late years
fallen under such great discouragements that they are unable to
improve or carry on the sugar trade upon an equal footing with
the foreign sugar colonies without some advantage and relief be
given to them from Great Britain: for remedy whereof, and for
the good and welfare of your Majesty's subjects, we your
Majesty's most dutiful and loyal subjects, the commons of Great
Britain assembled in parliament *have given and granted unto your
Majesty the several and respective rates and duties* herein after
mentioned.[3]

The act laid duties on the importation of molasses, sugar, and rum
from foreign sugar colonies. The duty on sugar was five shillings per
hundredweight, on rum, ninepence per gallon. But the most important duty was that of sixpence per gallon of imported molasses, such
a high level as to effectively prohibit its importation. An additional
economic burden was that the duties were required to be paid in
specie, in sterling "money of Great Britain."[4] The term of the statute
was five years; it was renewed from time to time after 1738.

The true purpose of the act was ambiguous, beginning with the
title. It was a carryover from proposed bills of 1731 and 1732 that
were intended to end the trade. The earlier bills had levied no duties
but instead explicitly had prohibited the trade, had forbidden the importation of molasses, sugar, and rum from foreign sugar colonies.[5]
Those earlier bills had passed the House of Commons, but the House
of Lords refused consent, seeing the prohibition as unnecessarily in-
terfering with trade of the empire. In order to obtain the effect of a

prohibition without being blocked in the Lords, the sponsors of the trade regulation decided to restructure the bill in such a manner that by imposing duties it had the form of a revenue act, thereby calling for the House of Lords to defer to the wishes of the House of Commons.

This duplicitous action, and conflicting statements during debate in the House of Commons (claiming it to be a revenue act, a *money bill*, rather than a regulation of trade), called into question the true intent of the act. For example, on March 8, debate dealt with the issue of whether the bill was a revenue measure or a trade regulation. Sir John Barnard moved to bring up a petition from Rhode Island against the bill. Thomas Winnington objected. "It has been a custom always observed in this House, not to receive any petitions against those Bills which were brought in for the laying on of any new duties." Barnard made a sharp response.

> Granting that it were a constant and perpetual rule not to receive petitions against such duties, yet certainly that rule could relate only to those duties, which were to be laid on for raising money for the current service of the public, it could not be presumed to relate to those duties, which were to be laid on for the regulation of trade only; and this last is the case now before us.

It was inappropriate to treat the bill as a revenue measure; no one expects, or even wishes, "that any money shall be thereby raised for the use of the public."

> The Bill is not intended for any such end; it is rather in the nature of a prohibition, and it was never pretended that no petitions were ever to be received against a Bill for prohibiting any sort of commerce.

After further debate along these lines, "the question was put for bringing up the petition, which passed in the negative." This refusal to bring up the petition put the imprimatur of the House of Commons on the bill: a revenue measure.[6]

In addition to the troubled history, the very words of the act make it unclear as to whether the statute is a regulation of trade or is intended to raise revenue. Its title has to do with trade, but the duties are "given and granted" to the King. The words *giving* and *granting* are words of donation, words of art in contract terms, a phrase that is one indication of a revenue act. (In fact, this is the first statute dealing with America that contains such words of donation.)

What was the purpose of this act? Prohibition? Revenue? The ambiguity was long lasting and worthy of learned comments from politicians and essayists. In 1774, Edmund Burke asserted in the House of Commons that the title was more important than the words of the preamble. "The title of this Act of George the 2nd, notwithstanding the words of donation, considers it merely as a regulation of trade."[7] Pamphleteer John Lind, writing on behalf of the government, expressed a different view. He criticized Burke's analysis and asserted that the words of donation did make this an act of revenue. "The act uses the technical words of 'give, and grant.' Here then at least, one would think, was clearly a duty imposed for the purpose of raising a revenue."[8] I have gone on at length about this issue, and about the long-lasting controversy, because the ambiguity will—in 1763, 1764, and later—affect American perception about the nature of additional statutes that combine the regulation of trade with the levy of duties for revenue.

American merchants thought the sixpence duty on foreign molasses imports was exorbitant, effectively a prohibition. But in the event, the molasses duty never did much to restrict American commerce; through bribery and smuggling the Americans imported the molasses they needed—at a cost of about one penny per gallon. The strategy was successful, largely since British leaders (during the long period later called "salutary neglect") made little effort to force compliance with the act.

PART ONE

Before Taxation

For over a century, British colonial policy was based on control of trade: products, sources, destinations, shipping. The policy was defined by the laws of trade, the Navigation Acts. This policy allowed Great Britain to become wealthy and powerful, raising revenue through duties collected at British ports and based on monopoly pricing by British merchants.[1]

Taxation played little part in colonial policy before 1764. There was no doubt in the minds of British leaders that Parliament always had the authority to levy taxes; it had chosen not to do so, an important factor being the economically undeveloped state of the colonies. However, by the end of the Seven Years' War in 1763, it was becoming clear that the Americans had become economically mature and even relatively wealthy. The British then embarked on a course that involved use of the laws of trade to draw revenue from America and—although not yet visible to the colonies—to institute parliamentary taxation.[2]

Chapter 1 explains the nature of the new policy and notification provided to Americans in 1763. The aspect of the policy revealed in that year dealt only with enforcement of the laws of trade and collection of customs duties. To the Americans, the expressed intent to strictly enforce the laws, and the instructions to the colonial governors to support such enforcement, sounded like a repeat of the empty rhetoric of the previous thirty years.

Chapter 2 details the American reaction: petitions and pamphlets developed as protests to the planned enforcement and collection of import duties on products from the West Indies. It is worthy of note that the resulting documents were protests of early 1764, before renewal of the Sugar Act of 1733.

One

A New Colonial Policy

"The sad story of colonial oppression commenced in the year 1764. Great Britain then adopted new regulations respecting her colonies, which, after disturbing the ancient harmony of the two countries for about twelve years, terminated in a dismemberment of the empire."

—David Ramsay, 1789

IN 1764, THE GOVERNMENT OF GREAT BRITAIN IMPLEMENTED A new colonial policy. The British added direct parliamentary taxation of America to the long-standing policy of control of colonial trade. Decisions by British leaders in 1763 at the end of the Seven Years' War informally coalesced into policy by the end of the year. The change was subtle: there was no proclamation by the king, no orders from the Privy Council, no record of a vote in the cabinet council, no statute passed by Parliament.[1]

The first component of the new policy was use of the laws of trade for the purpose of revenue. This was a change of policy, "where the dominant motive was not regulation and development, but regulation for the sake of revenue and political exploitation."[2] To outward appearance, the change appeared to be simply a modification of the long-standing policy of using customs duties to coax trade into desirable channels. The second component of the new policy was simple, unadorned taxation: stamp duties.[3] Driven by the decisions made in 1763, it was in 1764 that the policy began to take effect. As a consequence, it was in 1764 that the Americans began to reevaluate their constitutional relationship with Great Britain and, particularly, the relative authority of Parliament and of colonial legislatures.

INITIAL DECISIONS

To understand what happened in 1764, we must begin with the decisions made by British leaders in 1763. The end of the Seven Years' War, formally settled in February, brought profound changes to the relationship between Great Britain and America. Victorious Great Britain was ceded extensive territory in North America by France and Spain.

In order to secure this new territory, British leaders decided to retain a large peacetime garrison in North America: regiments of the British regular army, a total of 7,500 troops. Perhaps *decided* is too decisive a word. No formal decision was ever made, certainly not documented. No one even asked the question; it was simply assumed by all those in power that a British army for defense and protection was necessary. The rationale for the army was, first, to defend the North American colonies from French attempts to reconquer the ceded territory, and, second, to protect colonists from Native Americans, and vice versa. Great Britain, deep in debt and its people heavily taxed because of the war, needed the Americans to provide financial support for those forces. At the same time, British leaders decided the time was right to tighten up enforcement of the laws of trade, both to improve collection of revenue and to more closely bind the American colonies into the British Empire. The needs were so pressing that even before the end of the war, ideas "were in the air" regarding, "an army for the colonies, a colonial revenue to support it, and reform of colonial government."[4]

THE GRENVILLE PROGRAM

In April, George Grenville became First Lord of the Treasury and prime minister. It fell to Grenville's administration to deal with the decisions made earlier in the year. The first documented action to implement postwar policy was taken by Secretary of State Lord Egre-mont on May 5. He instructed the Board of Trade and Plantations to report how (among many other issues) the colonies could, with the least financial hardship, contribute to the expense of the regular British forces retained in America. The Lords Commissioners for Trade and Plantations responded on June 8, offering no recommen-dation for how the colonies might make such a contribution, claim-ing it was entirely out of their power to form any opinion.

On June 1, the Privy Council directed implementation of the Hov-ering Act, a statute passed earlier in the year that was designed to prevent smugglers from hovering off the coast looking for a place to land illegal cargo. The act had the effect of empowering officers of the Royal Navy to act as customs officials. On June 21, the Lords of the Admiralty wrote commanders of ships in the American fleet, or-dering them to "seize and proceed to condemnation of all such Ships and Vessels as you shall find offending against the said laws." In ad-dition, the Admiralty ordered additional vessels to join the fleet in American waters. And on July 9, Egremont directed colonial gover-nors to support enforcement of the laws of trade.[5]

Throughout June and July, the Treasury requested information from the Commissioners of Customs. Why did the customs duties levied in America fail to produce the expected revenue? What actions ought to be taken to improve collection of the duties? Among the points made in response were:

Appointed customs officers should be compelled to reside in America. (Many such customs officials simply continued to reside in Britain, delegating authority and workload to poorly paid deputies in the colonies.)

So long as the high duties on foreign molasses are continued, smuggling will be unavoidable.

Grenville took action to force customs officials to reside in Amer-ica. And it was about this time that he began to make decisions about revisions to the Sugar Act of 1733 (which, in any event, was due for renewal). The revisions would reduce the molasses duty, add more dutied products, appropriate the revenue to a specific purpose, and more. The decision process would take the rest of the year, even the early months of 1764.[6]

Grenville sent a comprehensive report to the Privy Council on October 4. This report is important—even famous—as it provided the basis for the revised Sugar Act.

> We the Commissioners of your Majesty's Treasury beg leave humbly to represent to your Majesty that having taken into consideration the present state of the duties of customs imposed on your Majesty's subjects in America and the West Indies, we find that the *revenue arising therefrom is very small and inconsiderable, having in no degree increased with the commerce of those countries, and is not yet sufficient to defray a fourth part of the expense necessary for collecting it.* We observe with concern that through neglect, connivance, and fraud, not only is revenue impaired, but the commerce of the colonies diverted from its natural Course and the salutary Provisions of many wise Laws to secure it to the Mother Country are in great Measure defeated.

There is an even broader issue about America.

> Attention to Objects of so great Importance, we are sensible is at all times our Duty, but at this it is more indispensable when the Military Establishment necessary for maintaining these Colonies requires a large Revenue to support it, and when their vast *Increase in Territory and Population makes the proper Regulation of their Trade of immediate Necessity,* lest the continuance and extent of the dangerous Evils abovementioned may render all Attempts to remedy them hereafter infinitely more difficult, if not utterly impracticable.

That sort of assertion suggests that British actions are not strictly the result of concern for raising revenue in the colonies but for strengthening the ties binding the colonies to Great Britain. Grenville explains the actions he has already taken to "remove the Causes to which the Deficiency of this Revenue . . . are owning."

We have ordered all the Officers belonging to the Customs in America and the West Indies to be fully instructed in their Duty, to repair forthwith to their respective stations, and constantly to reside there for the future.

But there were some things he needed the king to accomplish.

Strict Orders should be given to the Governors of all the Colonies to make the suppression of the clandestine and prohibited trade with foreign nations [a high priority, and] to give the Officers of the Revenue the necessary protection and Support.

The various suggestions continue, ending with a proposal for expanded jurisdiction of courts of admiralty in order to establish "a new and better method of condemning Seizures made in the Colonies."

The Officers of the Revenue when they have made a Seizure cannot but be under great doubt and Uncertainty, in what manner they should proceed to the condemnation of it. It is therefore humbly submitted to Your Majesty whether from the Importance of this Object it would not be of the greatest Public Utility, that an Uniform Plan be prepared for establishing the Judicature of the Courts of Admiralty in that Country.

On October 5, the Privy Council issued an Order in Council as complete acceptance of—and direction to implement—the report from Grenville.

The following memorial of 4 Oct. from the Treasury is approved, and the Earl of Halifax, Secretary of State, the Admiralty, and the Board of Trade instructed to give directions in accordance therewith.[7]

As part of Grenville's preparation for the renewal and revision of the Sugar Act, he realized that customs duties alone would not provide sufficient revenue.[8] He therefore decided to also levy stamp duties as they were used in Great Britain. He initiated action to prepare for both the introduction of the revised Sugar Act and a draft bill to implement a Stamp Act.[9]

INFORMING AMERICA: DUTIES TO BE COLLECTED

In early 1763, colonial agents in London reported that the colonies were expected to pay the cost of the British army for North America. Official, if obscure, notification followed.

On March 23, Massachusetts agent Jasper Mauduit wrote that Charles Townshend, the president of the Board of Trade, proposed lowering the duty on foreign molasses from sixpence to twopence in order to more effectively collect the duty. But only two weeks later, on April 8, Mauduit reported that "the Bill for lowering the Duty on French Molasses is put off till another Year."[10]

On May 30, the *New York Gazette* reported a letter from London dated March 27.

> I cannot omit mentioning a matter much the subject of conversation here, and which, if carried into execution, will in its consequences greatly affect the colonies. It is the quartering sixteen regiments in America, to be supported at the expense of the provinces. The inutility of these troops in time of peace, though evidently apparent, might not be complained of by the people of America, were the charge defrayed by England. But to lay that burthen on the plantations, already exhausted by the prosecution of an expensive war, is what I believe you would not have thought of. The money, it is said, will be levied by Act of Parliament, and *raised on a stamp duty* . . . and a duty on foreign sugar and molasses, &c. by reducing the former duty on these last-mentioned articles, which it is found impracticable to collect, to such a one as will be collected.

The writer is not much concerned with duties on foreign sugar and molasses but does express dread of taxes other than customs duties.

> This manner of raising money, except what may arise on the foreign sugars, &c., I apprehend, will be thought greatly to diminish

even the appearance of the subject's liberty, since nothing seems
to be more *repugnant to the general principles of freedom than
the subjecting a people to taxation by laws in the enactment of
which they are not represented.*[11]

The bland acceptance of the duties brings up a matter central to
the controversy of 1764. Americans accept that Parliament has the
right to regulate trade of the colonies, including placing duties on
foreign products, but the levy of stamp duties is "repugnant to the
general principles of freedom."

NOTIFICATION OF THE NEW POLICY

The first official notice of Grenville's intent to strictly enforce the
laws of trade was a circular letter to colonial governors from Secretary of State Egremont. It arrived in Boston on September 15.

> July 9, 1763
> Sir,
> It having appeared, that the Publick Revenue has been greatly di-
> minished, and the fair Trader much prejudiced, by the fraudulent
> Methods used to introduce into His Majesty's Dominions . . .
> Commodities of Foreign Growth, in National, as well as Foreign,
> Bottoms, by means of small Vessels hovering on the Coasts; And
> that this iniquitous Practice has been carried to a great Heighth
> in America; an Act was passed the last Session of Parliament, in-
> tituled, *An Act for the further Improvement of His Majesty's Rev-
> enue of Customs; And for the Encouragement of Officers making
> Seizures, and for the Prevention of the Clandestine Running of
> Goods into any Part of His Majesty's Dominions*; by which the
> former Laws, relative to this Matter, are enforced, and extended
> to the British Dominions in all Parts of the World.

The act referred to by Egremont is the Hovering Act. Eventually,
he gets to the action required: the governors are directed "to put an
effectual Stop to the clandestine Running of Goods into any place
within your Jurisdiction."

> The King wishes that all possible Means should be used to root
> out so iniquitous a Practice; a Practice carried on in Contravention
> of many express & repeated Laws, [leading] to the *Diminution &*
> *Impoverishment of the Public Revenue.*

Egremont goes on, explaining other enforcement actions taken by
the ministry, and enclosing the Hovering Act and other information.
At the end, he further emphasizes the importance to the king of "Improvement of the Public Revenue." It is a matter on which "His
Majesty lays so much stress." That Egremont repeatedly emphasizes
improving the revenue is a clue that something new is going on. The
letter hints that the direction from the king is not simply another
empty exhortation to adhere to the laws of trade that the governors
have been hearing for the past thirty years.[12]
   Massachusetts governor Francis Bernard was out of town when
the circular letter arrived, so the first British official in Massachusetts
to see it was Lieutenant Governor Thomas Hutchinson. He discussed
the letter when writing the politically well-connected Richard Jackson on September 17. (Jackson was London agent for Connecticut
and Pennsylvania, legal counsel to the Massachusetts agents, and
later a Massachusetts agent himself.)[13]

> I wonder we heard nothing of the Act of Parliament giving new
> powers to the Comanders of His Majestys Ships for seizing illicit
> traders. The first intelligence was from the Act itself & [the Egre-
> mont letter]. I fancy many of the West India traders will be sur-
> prized.

Hutchinson recognizes, and knows that Jackson will understand,
that the new stress on enforcement to draw revenue from duties is
largely about the American trade with sugar islands in the West Indies.

> Such indulgence has been shewn of late to that branch of illicit
> trade that no body has considered it as such, vessels arriving &
> making their entries for some small acknowledgments as openly
> as from our own Islands & without paying the duties.[14]

Governor Bernard returned, and responded to Egremont on October 25.

> Ever since I have been in this Government, I have exerted the best of my powers to maintain a due obedience to the [applicable] Laws; and I can with pleasure add, that I beleive they are no where better supported than they are in this province.[15]

Bernard drones on and on but never reveals his concerns about decisions being made in London. He did share his apprehension with John Pownall, secretary to the Board of Trade. (By 1763, the Sugar Act of 1733 was on and off referred to as the Molasses Act.)

> October 30, 1763
> The People here are greatly alarmed at a report that it is determined to carry the Molasses Act into full Execution. I could write a Volume against this measure if I was at Liberty, but I dont think it prudent to obtrude my advice, especially as it is probable that the contrary to it is resolved upon. So that I will only say, & that in Confidence to you, that I dread the Consequence of such a resolution.
>   It can't be imagined that NAmerica will be sacrificed at this time of day to the West Indies; *and therefore the only motive to such a stop is supposed to be the raising a good sum of money.*

He sees the need for a drastically lower duty on molasses.

> But it is my opinion paradoxical as it may seem, that more mony could be raised by a penny a Gallon than by Six pence. And tho' possibly the trade may bear, three half pence, it would be better to set out with a penny tho' it was determined to add another half penny soon after. For this reason if there was no other: everyone will readily submit to one penny tho' it is to be doubted whether three half pence will be so well received.[16]

The Board of Trade, following direction of the Order in Council of October 5, called for strict enforcement with a circular letter to all governors. Governor Bernard received the instructions in December.

October 11, 1763
The Lords Commissioners of His Majesty's Treasury having represented to His Majesty that they find upon a consideration of the present state of the Duties of Customs imposed on His Majesty's Subjects in America, *that the Revenue arising therefrom is very small & inconsiderable, having in no degree increased with the Commerce of those Countries, and is not yet sufficient to defray a fourth part of the expence necessary for collecting it*, and that through neglect connivance & fraud, not only the Revenue is impaired, but the Commerce of the Colonies is diverted from it's natural course, & the salutary provisions of many wise Laws are in great measure defeated.

The board directs vigorous action.

His Majesty has commanded us to require & enjoin you in the strictest manner to make the Suppresion of the clandestine & prohibited Trade with foreign Nations, *& the improvement of the Revenue* the constant & immediate Objects of your care; & by a vigorous discharge of the Duty required of you by several Acts of Parliament, and a due execution of your legal Authority, to give the Officers of the Revenue all possible protection & Support.[17]

Bernard responded on December 26. He claimed "no neglect that I know of in executing the laws of trade within this province." However, "the Melesses Act [has] never been duly executed; altho' at the same time I must, for my own defence, say, that I never knew an instance of the breach of it." But there is a problem with ambiguity.

This act has been a perpetual stumbling block to Customhouse officers: and it will be most agreeable to them to have it anyways removed. The Question seems to be *whether it should be an act of prohibition or an act of revenue.*

His analysis:

It was originally, I believe, designed for the former; and if it shall be thought advisable to continue it as such, it will want no more than to be fully executed. But if it is meant to be an Act of Revenue, the best means to make it Effectual, that is to raise the greatest Revenue by it, will be to lower the Duties in such a proportion as will secure the entire collection of them & encourage the importation of the goods on which they will be laid.

That the Molasses Act was intended as prohibition was the universal understanding in America; it influenced the American protests we will see in chapter 2 and all the later colonial protests dealing with customs duties.

It is, in my opinion, a false state of this Question, to consider it as a Contest between the West Indies & North America: it is really a contest between the West Indies & Great Britain; . . . The Trade of North America is really the Trade of Great Britain.

And perhaps his most compelling reason against enforcement: "America will suffer for a time only . . . But the Loss to Great Britain will be irretrievable."[18]

FURTHER TAXATION

By late 1763, it was clear that Grenville was going to call for a tax to support British troops in America and that such a tax was going to be passed by Parliament. A complex part of the consequent controversy over taxation has to do with the distinction between customs duties (often called port duties) and internal taxes such as stamp duties. This issue was brought up by Richard Jackson. On December 27, he wrote to Benjamin Franklin (who was then a member of the Pennsylvania committee of correspondence).

A Revenue to be raised in America for the Support of British Troops is not now to [be] argued against: it would answer no Purpose to do so. I only contend that it should be built on a foundation consistent with the Constitutions of the Colonies, and on the Principles of Relation between the Mother Countries and her Colonies. It is not disputed that [each Mother Country] is Mistress of the Trade of its Colonys: this Right has always been challenged and exercised by England and all other Countries; [since the Mother Country] may prohibit foreign Trade, it may therefore tax it. And the Colonys have a Compensation in Protection, *but I dread internal Taxes.*[19]

Jackson recognizes the authority of Parliament to regulate trade ("prohibit foreign trade"), even pointing out that it has the right to tax the trade. The wording is tricky here. What Jackson is referring to as a tax on foreign trade is a customs duty. Indeed, customs duties are sometimes referred to as taxes—specifically external taxes—and are acceptable to Americans. (Acceptable despite the fact that Americans consistently and universally reject taxation. I did say the wording is tricky.)[20]

The following letter from Jasper Mauduit is intended to bring the Massachusetts General Court up to date. Mauduit has the same perception as Jackson, that Parliament is committed to raising a revenue from America.

December 30, 1763

All agree, that a practicable duty should be laid, and the payment of it enforced. To attempt to controvert either of these, would be to no manner of purpose. As the *general court have not been pleased to instruct me* in their sentiments upon this subject, I was left to pursue my own, in conjunction with the other agents. And *their silence inclined me to think, that such a scheme, if duly moderated, might not be disagreeable,* though they might not choose to appear openly to oppose it. The sum at first thought of by the treasury was 4d. [4 pennies, or four pence] but Mr. Grenville seems to be now satisfied with two pence.

(We will later see that he has misread the silence of the General Court.)

We are endeavouring at a penny; it will not be more than two pence. All that the duty can be brought to, under that, must be reckoned as gain. There are many other regulations intended, about which I find that the gentlemen in parliament have very different ideas. I hope, however, there will be found a general disposition to serve the colonies, and not to distress them.[21]

On January 26, 1764, Jackson wrote Franklin to further inform him of goings-on in London.

Measures are taken for bringing several American Questions before Parliament. They are so numerous that I am quite at a loss where to begin, and I am so employd not only in attending the House, but in combating what I deem the most dangerous Errors in American Politicks in 100 Places.

As he indicated in the earlier letter, he is sure taxation is on the way.

I have long since given up all hopes of preventing some Parliamentary Tax to be imposed on N America as well as the W Indies for the maintenance of the Troops kept there.

His concern is for the form of taxation, again showing concern about an internal tax.

I am most averse to an Internal Tax; God knows how far such a precedent may be extended, and I have frequently asked, what internal Tax they will not lay.

Since he is resigned to taxation by Parliament, what sort of taxation is acceptable?

Customs [i.e., port duties], as well as Prohibitions on Trade, have been at all times, laid by England from the time of the long Parliament. I wish this to be the Rule of Conduct on this Occasion.[22]

He wishes to see the "Parliamentary Tax to be imposed" as a port duty, an external tax. In this sense an external tax is not quite a customs duty but is a revenue duty levied on goods being imported and collected at the port. He believes this to be within the rightful authority of Parliament.

BEGINNING ENFORCEMENT

By late 1763, the enforcement actions of the Grenville administration earlier in the year were having a troublesome effect on American shipping. Governor Bernard, writing Richard Jackson on November 26, explains the situation.

> The Merchants here are greatly alarmed at the present proceedings to guard this Coast & especially the appointing the Captains of the men of War to be Customhouse Officers. [The merchants] are strange People; they are either for taking the government by Storm & enforcing such a remission of the laws of trade as they think fit; or else in a fit of Despondency they give up themselves & their trade to ruin. They never think of a middle way, to remonstrate, with decency, upon the real hardships they lay under & to crave redress, which I cannot think would be hard to obtain.[23]

Neither Bernard nor the merchants recognized as yet that a change of colonial policy was in the wind.

Eventually, high-level decisions and commands reached the officials charged with putting them into execution, causing orders to be issued for strict enforcement of the Molasses Act (ending the previous lax policy). Here is the announcement from the Collector of the Port of Boston.

> *Boston Evening-Post*, January 2, 1764
> Whereas it has been represented to the Right Honourable the Lords Commissioners of His Majesty's Treasury, that many Vessels trading to the Plantations not belonging to the King of Great Britain, and returning with Cargoes of Rum, Sugar, and Molasses, have found Means to smuggle the same into his Majesty's Colonies, without paying the King's Duty. This is to inform all

Masters of Vessels using the said Trade, that they are hereby strictly required on their Arrival here, to enter or report their Ships and Cargoes at the Custom House, when proper Officers will be put on board such Vessels, to see that the Act of the Sixth of his late Majesty King George the Second (imposing a Duty on all foreign Rum, Sugar, and Molasses) be in all it's Parts *fully carried into Execution.*
By Order of the Surveyor-General,
R. Hale, Collector[24]

(In later chapters, we will hear more from the surveyor-general, John Temple.) Officials at other ports in the northern colonies made similar announcements.

On January 7, 1764, Bernard wrote Jackson.

The publication of orders for the strict execution of the Melasses Act has caused a [great] alarm in this Country. . . . Petitions from the trading Towns have been presented to the general Court, and a large committee of both houses is setting every day to prepare instructions for their Agent. In the Mean time the Merchants say, there is an end of the trade of this Province; that it is sacrificed to the West Indian Planters.[25]

Although the Americans were coming to the realization that the Molasses Act was, in fact, this time going to be enforced, there was still no realization that the enforcement was simply the opening scene of a soon-to-be-enacted constitutional drama.

Two

America Protests
Enforcement

BASED ON REPORTS EARLY IN 1763 FROM MASSACHUSETTS AGENT Jasper Mauduit, Boston merchants were apprehensive ("fears had been aroused of a renewal") about British plans for the Sugar Act.[1] On April 14, 1763, the merchants formally organized "the Society for Encouraging Trade and Commerce within the Province of Massachusetts Bay." The "immediate purpose of the Society was to prevent the renewal" of the Sugar Act.[2] The merchants took no action to prevent renewal until late in the year, but their writings and letters to like-minded colonies then prompted further protest.

REASONS AGAINST THE RENEWAL OF THE SUGAR ACT
In December, the Boston merchants drew up a memorial stating reasons against renewal. It was presented to the Massachusetts General Court on December 27, "praying that his Excellency and Honors would take into Consideration the Act of Parliament known by the Name of the Sugar Act . . . and make such Application for their Relief as they in their great Wisdom shall judge best."[3]

As the Act, commonly called the Sugar Act, has been passed upwards of thirty years without any Benefit to the Crown, the Duties arising from it, having never been appropriated by Parliament to any particular Use; and as this Act will expire this Winter, the following Considerations are offered as Reasons why it should not be renewed.

Enforcement of the act will put an end to all trade with the foreign islands.

FIRST, It is apprehended that the Trade is so far from being able to bear the high Duties imposed by this Act, *that it will not bear any Duty at all.*

Although the idea "that it will not bear any Duty at all" was echoed by other colonies, as a practical matter it was understood that a low molasses duty would be acceptable—it would not interfere with trade to the foreign islands and would be offset by saving the expense of smuggling or bribery.

[At the current cost of molasses] it will barely answer to distil it into Rum for Exportation. Should this Duty be added, it would have the *Effect of an absolute Prohibition* on the Importation of Molasses and Sugar from the foreign Islands; and consequently the same effect on the Exportation of Fish, Lumber and other Commodities from hence to those Islands; as the French, Dutch and other Foreigners whom we supply with those Articles, *will not permit us to bring away their Money; so that unless we can take their ordinary Sugars and Molasses in Return, this Trade will be lost.*

Fishing is a vital industry. It stands on two legs: high-quality fish to Europe and less-desirable fish to the West Indies. Neither side of the business can stand alone.

SECONDLY, The Loss of the Trade to the foreign Islands, on which great Part of our other Trade depends, must greatly affect all the Northern Colonies, and entirely destroy the Fishery in this Province.

Since the British sugar islands take only a small portion of the undesirable fish, "the Remainder will be lost if we are prevented from supplying the foreign Islands, there being no other Market where it can be disposed of."

THIRDLY, A Prohibition on the Trade to foreign Islands will greatly promote the French Fishery: If the French Islands can be supplied with Fish for Molasses, it will be cheaper for them to purchase it of us than to catch it themselves.

But if American merchants cannot profitably trade fish for molasses, the French will expand their own fishery. And "their establishing such a Fishery will be very prejudicial to Great Britain."

FOURTHLY, The Fishery being a great Nursery of Seamen for his Majesty's Navy, the Destruction thereof must very much weaken the Naval Power of Great Britain.

And there are other adverse consequences. Trade of Great Britain.

FIFTHLY, The Destruction of the Fishery will be very prejudicial to the Trade of Great Britain by lessening the Demand for her Manufactures.

Trade of the colonies.

SIXTHLY, The Destruction of the Fishery will not only lessen the Importation of Goods from Great Britain, but must greatly prejudice the whole Trade of the Province. The Trade to the foreign Islands is become very considerable, [they being] supplied with Provisions, Fish, Lumber, Horses, Onions and other Articles exported from the Northern Colonies; for which we receive Molasses in Return; this is distilled into Rum for the Fishery, and to export to the Southern Colonies.

Further, rum is vital for the trade with Africa, "to purchase Slaves for our own Islands in the West-Indies."[4]

It is said by the Planters in the West-Indies that they can supply us with Rum and Molasses for the Fishery, and our own Consumption. . . . To which it may be answered [no they cannot].

Economy of the colonies.

SEVENTHLY, The Destruction of the Fishery will be the Ruin of those concerned in that Business, and that are dependent on it.

The king's revenue.

EIGHTHLY, The Sugar Act, if put in Execution, will greatly affect the King's Revenue, by lessening the Importation of Rum and Sugar into Great Britain. The Duties paid upon Rum, it is said, amount to upwards of £50,000 Sterling per Annum; this will be wholly lost to the Crown, as the Northern Colonies will take all the Rum our Islands can make; consequently none can be shipped to Great Britain.

The Sugar Act works to benefit only a privileged few.

NINTHLY, This Act was procured by the Interest of the West-India Planters, with no other View than to enrich themselves by obliging the northern Colonies to take their whole Supply from them.

The memorial ends with a summary of the situation, and a view of the future.

Upon the whole, It is plain that our Islands are able neither to supply us with what we want from them, nor to take from us what Lumber and Fish we are obliged to export: and they will be still less able to do either; for our Demands will be growing faster than their Produce, and our Fishery which has been increasing, will

continue still to increase, if not obstructed, while their Demands
have not increased in any Proportion, and never can.⁵

On January 4, 1764, the Boston merchants wrote their counterparts in Rhode Island (and five days later, Connecticut) referring to
the memorial as the *State of the Trade.*

The Act commonly known by the Name of the Sugar Act has long
& justly been complain'd of by the Northern Colonies as a great
Grievance; and should it be continued & put in Execution, with
any Degree of Rigour (as is like to be the Case hereafter) it will
give a mortal Wound to the Peace of these Colonies.

   As this Act is now about to expire, it behoves us all to unite
our endeavors to prevent, if possible, the revival of it.

   To this Purpose the Merchants in this Town, sometime since,
met together and chose a Committee to prepare a *State of the
Trade* of this Province so far as it is affected by this act.

They explain that the Massachusetts General Court "will send the
necessary Instructions to their Agent, and will oppose the Renewal
of the Act to the utmost of their Power." They enclose the "State of
the Trade," and look for assistance "in our Endeavours to defeat the
iniquitous Schemes of these overgrown West Indians." In addition
to actions of the General Court, "the Merchants here will severally
write to their respective Correspondents in England & endeavour to
convince them that the Act in Question is and will be prejudicial to
the Trade of Great Britain."⁶

   In the weeks following presentation to the General Court, the memorial was refined (principally in minor rephrasing), then printed as
a pamphlet: *Reasons against the renewal of the Sugar Act as it will
be prejudicial to the trade, not only of the northern colonies, but to
that of Great-Britain also.* The body of the pamphlet was preceded
by an advertisement.

The Reasons offered in the following Pages against the Renewal
of the Act of Parliament, imposing a Duty on foreign Sugar and
Molasses imported into the British Colonies, are founded princi-

pally on the pernicious Effect this Act will have on the Trade of the Massachusetts Province in particular, and the Detriment which will hereby accrue to the Trade and Manufactures of Great Britain.

In the only substantive change to the memorial as presented to the General Court, the ending of the pamphlet was expanded by preceding the final paragraph with a summary of the reasons against renewal.

Upon the whole, it is evident that the renewal of this act, will be followed by the most pernicious consequences. Instead of encreasing, it will sink the king's revenue. It will weaken the naval power of Great Britain, by destroying our fishery, that great nursery of British seamen, and at the same time, it will strengthen the marine of France, by encouraging the French fishery. It will be highly prejudicial to the trade of Britain, and even destructive to that of these colonies: for our islands are able neither to supply us . . . [and so on, as in the memorial].[7]

On February 10, the merchants sent 250 copies of the pamphlet to their counterparts in London. The pamphlet also was sent to other towns in Massachusetts and to neighboring colonies. Local distribution drew commentary from Governor Bernard; he wrote John Pownall on February 10, "I send you herewith some printed papers about the Melasses Act; the stitchd piece is the produce of this Town, but, tho containing a good deal of matter, it's not in my opinion very judiciously handled."[8]

As it turns out, the pamphlet did not arrive in London until it was too late to influence the debates on the Sugar Act of 1764. In fact, for a variety of reasons, none of the essays, petitions, or pamphlets of early 1764 reached London in time to influence the passage of the new Sugar Act. This did not mean that Grenville was unaware of the American opposition to the renewal; the agents presented (somewhat lackadaisically for the most part) the arguments.

The best representation of the American position was developed by Israel Mauduit (the brother and informal, unpaid assistant of

Massachusetts agent Jasper Mauduit). Based on discussion throughout 1763, and especially on letters with guidance from Thomas Cushing (a patriot leader and influential member of the Massachusetts
General Court), he prepared a document that was submitted to the
Treasury by Jasper Mauduit: *A Memorial to the Lords Commissioners of His Majesty's Treasury*. The memorial, which was signed by
other colonial agents, did not attempt to prevent the renewal; it instead put forth arguments that in order to allow unhampered trade,
no more than one penny per gallon should be assessed. (But, defer-
ring to the judgment of the Treasury, the memorial allowed that two
pennies would be acceptable.)[9] The memorial was presented to and
rejected by the Treasury on February 27. That was the last gasp of
protests from the agents; they reached an understanding that further
protest would antagonize and discourage friends of America in the
House of Commons.

AN ESSAY ON THE TRADE OF THE NORTHERN COLONIES

The *Providence* (RI) *Gazette*, on January 14 and 21, published an
anonymous essay laying out the harmful effect of the Sugar Act: *An
Essay on the Trade of the Northern Colonies of Great Britain in
North America.*

> The commerce of the British northern colonies in America is so
> peculiarly circumstanced, and from permanent causes, so per-
> plexed and embarrassed, that it is a business of great difficulty to
> investigate it, and put it in any tolerable point of light.
>   That which most particularly and unhappily distinguishes most
> of these northern British colonies from all others, either British or
> any other nation, is that the soil and climate of them is incapable
> of producing almost anything which will serve to send directly
> home to the mother country.

In addition, "their situation and circumstances are such as to be
obliged to take off, and consume [great] quantities of British Manufactures." Having almost nothing to directly trade, purchases from
Great Britain must be made with specie. The consequence is, "Unable
to make remittances in a direct way, they are obliged to do it by a

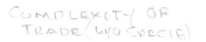

circuity of commerce unpracticed by and unnecessary in any other colony." When they cannot sell products for specie, they must be satisfied to "procure such things in return as may [require] several commercial exchanges to make a remittance home."

Exports start with fish from the northernmost colonies. The fish "that are called merchantable are sent directly to Spain, Portugal, and Italy, and there sold for money or bills of exchange, which are sent directly to England."

> A considerable part of the fish yet remaining, which is unfit for the European markets, serves for feeding the slaves in the West Indies; as much of this is sold in the English islands as they will purchase, and the residue sold in the French and Dutch Colonies, and in the end is turned into a remittance home.

"The colonies next to the southward" must rely on the circuity of commerce to transform exports into molasses, molasses into rum, and eventually into specie.

> Lumber, horses, pork, beef . . . [are] sold to the French and Dutch for molasses; *this molasses is brought into these colonies, and there distilled into rum*, which is sent to the coast of Africa, and there sold for gold, ivory, and slaves: the two first of these are sent directly home; the slaves are carried to the English West-Indies and sold for money or bills of exchange, which are also remitted to England.

None of the trade is "detrimental to the true interests of Great Britain, or in any degree injurious to the British sugar colonies." Such trade, "we reasonably expect will be totally prohibited." The essay provides a specific example of a "supposed injury" to the British planters, that the foreign trade raises the price of northern produce and lowers the price of their own. The retort to that charge is that trade with the French and Dutch is needed to acquire "money or melasses, neither of which the British sugar colonies have to spare." In fact, the British sugar islands are supplied with provisions "at fifty per cent less than the same kinds of goods are sold for to the French and Dutch." And when trading with the British colonies, the Americans pay more for products than they do from the French and Dutch.

After further long explanation, mixing in more problems of trade restriction, along the way disparaging "the rich, proud, and overbearing planters of the West Indies," the memorial turns to the duty, which should have been only a halfpenny per gallon. "As the trade might have borne such a duty it would have been chearfully paid by the merchants, and would even at this rate, produce a far greater revenue yearly to the crown than has ever yet been paid by all the continent in America."

Ultimately, the high duty reduces imports from Great Britain.

It may be depended on as an axiom, that nothing limits the consumption of British manufactures in the northern colonies, but the people's ability to pay for them; and that whatever lessens that ability will in the same proportion lessen the consumption.

The essay wraps things up on a high note, advising that the colonies not evade the law, and instead initiate united action appealing to the wonderful British government. "All the colonies concerned ought to unite, and appoint proper persons, who may prepare a true state of the commerce of these colonies." Such a "proper application to the British legislature [should be] sent to their several agents," laid before the Board of Trade, and eventually brought before Parliament.

If their cause be good, as most certainly it is, what have they to fear from such a procedure? Or rather, what have they not to hope from such an application and appeal to a king who delights in doing good to all his subjects; to a peerage, wise, and accurate, guided by the principles of honor and beneficence; and a representative body, penetrating and prudent, who consider the good of the whole, and make that the measure of their public resolves.[10]

Published anonymously, it later became known that Governor Stephen Hopkins of Rhode Island was the author. The essay was reprinted by newspapers in Boston, New York, and Philadelphia and later published as a pamphlet in London. The June 1764 issue of the

London *Monthly Review* was complimentary. "The subject of this Essay is of a very interesting nature, and treated in a masterly and judicious manner by one who appears to be perfectly well acquainted with it." And after a summary, it states that the essay "well deserves the candid Reader's attentive perusal."[11]

In the same letter of February 10 we saw earlier, in which Bernard was critical of the pamphlet *Reasons against the renewal of the Sugar Act*, he had a more positive comment on the essay by Hopkins. After saying that the Boston pamphlet was not "very judiciously handled," he commented on the Hopkins essay.

> The other is as you may observe, taken from a newspaper, which I have for convenience pasted together. It comes from Rhode Island & is said to be the work of an eminent Gentleman there; be it whose it will, it is sensible & methodical. . . . I send like copies to Jackson; whether I can add a letter to him will depend upon the Wind tomorrow. I have promist to finish my dispatches to night: but shall add to them if the Ship dont sail tomorrow.[12]

REMONSTRANCE AGAINST THE RENEWAL

Rhode Island merchants, prompted by the letter of January 4 from Boston, requested that Governor Hopkins call a special meeting of the General Assembly. The merchants needed little prompting; they were already concerned about enforcement and had already drafted preliminary essays explaining the economic problems caused by the Sugar Act. In addition, newspapers (in New York, Rhode Island, and Pennsylvania) had for months been full of news and opinions about the enforcement of the laws of trade and what action should be taken. "There can be no Doubt that upon a proper Representation to his Majesty and his Ministry, we shall have every just Cause of Complaint removed, and be allowed all the Advantages in Trade that we could reasonably ask."[13]

On January 13, the governor called for the General Assembly to meet on January 24. Between the call for the meeting and its convening, a committee of merchants prepared a remonstrance against the renewal. It was presented on January 26 and—approved by the General Assembly—became the first American legislative protest against renewal of the Sugar Act. The remonstrance was directed to the Board of Trade, from "the Governor and Company of the English colony of Rhode Island and Providence Plantations."

> Humbly show:
> That the act passed in the sixth year of the reign of His late Majesty George II, commonly called the sugar act, being to expire at the end of the present session of Parliament; and as the same, if continued, may be highly injurious and detrimental to all His Majesty's North American colonies in general, and to this colony in particular, the said Governor and Company presume to offer some considerations drawn from the particular state and circumstances of said colony, *against the renewal* of said act.

The remonstrance explains that the colony produces little to trade directly to the mother country. Nonetheless, the colony annually requires British manufactures in the "amount at least to £120,000, sterling." The goods available for export "will answer at no market but in the West Indies."

> It necessarily follows that the trade thither must be the foundation of all our commerce; and it is undoubtedly true, that solely from the prosecution of this trade with the other branches that are pursued in consequence of it, arises the ability to pay for such quantities of British goods.

The result of trade with the foreign islands is the "import into this colony about fourteen thousand hogsheads of molasses." But much less from the British islands, "a quantity not exceeding twenty-five hundred hogsheads." Molasses is central to the economy of the colony; it "serves as an engine in the hands of the merchant to effect the great purpose of paying for British manufactures." Part of the molasses is traded to other colonies; "the remainder (besides what is consumed by the inhabitants) is distilled into rum, and exported to the coast of Africa."

This little colony, only, for more than thirty years past, have annually sent about eighteen sail of vessels to the coast, which have carried about eighteen hundred hogsheads of rum, together with a small quantity of provisions and some other articles, which have been sold for slaves, gold dust, elephants' teeth, camwood, &c. The slaves have been sold in the English islands, in Carolina, and Virginia, for bills of exchange, and the other articles have been sent to Europe; and by this trade alone, remittances have been made from this colony to Great Britain, to the value of about £40,000 yearly.

The current cost of molasses is the highest at which "it can be distilled into rum for exportation." And payment of a duty in specie is impossible.

If a duty should be laid on this article, the enhanced price may amount to a prohibition; and it may with truth be said, *that there is not so large a sum of silver and gold circulating in the colony*, as the duty imposed by the aforesaid act upon foreign molasses, would amount to in one year, which makes it absolutely impossible for the importers to pay it.

The northern colonies must trade with the French and Dutch to export their products.

The British West India islands are not, nor in the nature of things, ever can be able to consume the produce of the [northern] colonies; and therefore, if [the northern colonies] cannot export it (which they never can, unless they are allowed to bring molasses home) a very great part of the produce of the said colonies must be entirely lost.

There are more tales of woe.

[Distilling rum is] the main hinge upon which the trade of the colony turns, and many hundreds of persons depend immediately upon it for a subsistence. These distil houses, for want of molasses, must be shut up, to the ruin of many families.

The remonstrance ends with a direct appeal to the Board of Trade.

> From the facts and arguments contained in the aforegoing repre-
> sentation, it is submitted to Your Lordships, whether the renewal
> of the said law may not, instead of answering any useful purposes,
> be highly injurious to the interest both of Great Britain and these
> northern colonies.[14]

On January 27, the General Assembly approved a letter to agent
Joseph Sherwood instructing him "to present the [Remonstrance] to
the Lords Commissioners for Trade and Plantations and take the
most effectual Measures in Conjunction with the Agents of the
Northern Colonies to Accomplish the Purpose intended by said Remonstrance."[15]

REMARKS ON THE TRADE OF THE COLONY

The Boston letter also prompted action from Connecticut merchants.
As in Rhode Island, the merchants needed little prompting; even be-
fore hearing from Boston, early news of enforcement "threw the
Connecticut importers into a panic."[16]

On January 20, the merchants presented a memorial to the Connecticut General Assembly that "his Majesty has been pleased of late
to Inforce the Execution of the Sugar Act," and that it "Expires about
this time & will probably be again revived unless prevented by a Sea-
sonable remonstrance on the part of the Northern Colonies." The
merchants requested that Connecticut join with other colonies in re-
monstrating against enforcement and renewal of the act.

The General Assembly took no timely action, but the merchants
published a pamphlet later in the month, *Remarks on the Trade of
the Colony.*

> As the Sugar Act comonly so cal'd expires this Winter, its the In-
> terest of the Northern Colonies to use their best Endeavours to
> prevent its being revived.
>   The Trade of the Colony of Connecticut consists in Shipbuild-
> ing . . . and Exportation of Beef, Pork . . . Rum, Sugar & Molasses
> to [neighboring] Provinces to pay for British Manufactures bought

of them for the Consumption of the Inhabitants of the Colonys and to purchase Codfish, Mackrel, and Oyle for the West India Market. Also in exporting Horses, Cattle, Sheep . . . to the English & Foreign Ports in the West Indies. And Rum distilled here to Africa to purchase Slaves for the West India Market, for all which we receive Rum, Sugar & Molasses in Return.

High import duties are a prohibition.

Should the [said] Sugar Act be reviv'd & put in full Execution, it will amount to a total prohibition of the Northern Colonies suplying any Foreign Port in the West Indies with those Articles, & the English Islands must consiquently be the only purchasers.

And that is a problem. "The supply [of horses, cattle, etc.] will be vastly more than those Islands have a demand for." There is a broader problem.

If the Trade from the Northern Colonies to Forreign Ports in the West Indies is prohibited, no one will deny that the French will open a Trade to Missisipi and Increase their Fishery, to Supply the French as well as the Spanish Dutch & Danish West Indies.

There is a political issue.

The Number of Inhabitants in the Northern Colonies when compared to the Inhabitants of the English West India Islands, are supos'd to be in proportion as Twenty to One, & notwithstanding the great superiority of the Northern Colonies in Number, they have not One Member in the British Parliament and the West India Islands have Fifty Six. Can this difference proceed from the Poverty of the Proprietors of the Sugar Islands, or from their Affluence, which solely arises from the Produce of their Sugar Plantations.

And a financial issue.

[It is not in] the Interest of Great Brittain that an Act of Parliament should be revivd to increase the Proffits ariseing to the Proprietors of the English Sugar Islands (already greater than any Land Holders in the Kings Dominons) when the damage will be so amazeingly great to the Northern Colonies . . . that it will leave at least one half their Navigation & Seamen unimploy'd, the demand for Shipbuilding will cease, the Land Holders, & Tradesmen be discourag'd, prevent the large importation of British Manufactures, & render the Colonies *unable to pay their Debts already contracted in Great Britain.*[17]

MEMORIAL IN OPPOSITION TO THE RENEWAL

New York merchants were also active in opposition to renewal of the Sugar Act. In February, they prepared a memorial in opposition to the renewal, requested that the General Assembly direct the agent "to go hand in hand with the other governments," and persuaded Lieutenant Governor Cadwallader Colden to forward the memorial to the Board of Trade. And they wrote to merchants in Philadelphia, explaining their actions and that they were "heartily joining the eastern governments in soliciting a discontinuance of the most unjust of all laws, the Sugar Act."[18]

The New York General Assembly acted on April 20.

Alderman Livingston, in Behalf of the Merchants of the City of New-York, laid before the house, a Copy of a Memorial, drawn up by the said Merchants, in order to be presented to the Parliament of Great Britain, complaining of the Hardships the Trade of this Colony labours under, by Reason of a Statute of the sixth of his late Majesty King George the Second, commonly called the Sugar Act; and praying Relief in the Premises.

Resolved, *Nemine Contradicente*, That the House do approve of the said Memorial.

To the Honourable the Knights, Citizens, and Burgesses, in Parliament assembled. The Memorial of the Merchants of the City of New-York, in the Colony of New-York, in America.

Humbly Sheweth,

That the declining State of the Commerce of this and the other Northern Colonies, from the present rigorous Executions of the Statute of the sixth of his late Majesty King George the Second, called the Sugar Act, is become an Object of such serious and universal Concern that [they cannot] remain silent Spectators of the impending Ruin.

After praising the "Impartiality, Justice, and Wisdom of the British Parliament," they express full confidence that Parliament will "effectually secure them an adequate Redress." The remainder of the memorial is a lengthy representation of why such redress should be granted. "The Soil produces little or nothing that affords" the ability to pay for British manufactures, thus forcing dependence on foreign trade.

The Suppression of their Trade with the foreign Sugar Islands . . . must necessarily end not only in the utter Impoverishment of his Majesty's Northern Colonies, and the Destruction of their Navigation, but in the grievous Detriment of the British Manufactures and Artificers, and the great Diminution of the Trade, Power, Wealth and naval Strength of Great Britain.

Reasons against renewal are advanced at great length, repeating the arguments of the other colonies; for example, "Flour, Beef, Pork, Lumber and Horses . . . [are] sold in the foreign Colonies, either for Specie, Sugar or Molasses," the specie being remitted to Great Britain. The New York economy is dependent upon a *course of trade*, what Hopkins in January had called the "circuity of commerce."

Sugar and Molasses have been shewn to be the very Sinews of our Commerce, and the Sources from which, in a Course of Trade, we draw the most valuable Remittances; it would therefore seem necessary that they should be imported in Quantities Sufficient to supply the various Demands of our several commercial Interchanges, as well as our own Consumption; but our Sugar Colonies are unable to afford this ample Supply, nor if they were, could they take of our Produce, which alone would capacitate us to purchase it.

The memorial ends with a long harangue rebutting past assertions of the West Indian planters.

The General Assembly took this additional action.

Ordered, That the Committee of Correspondence, direct the Agent of this Colony to give all possible *Opposition to the Renewal*, or Continuation, of the said Act of the sixth of his late Majesty King George the Second; and acquaint him, that this House will pay all such Expenses as may accrue by Means of the said Opposition.[19]

NATURE OF THE PROTESTS

The reasons advanced by the four northern colonies were the "first intercolonial movement of the pre-Revolutionary period designed to exert political pressure in England."[20] None of the five protests made an appeal to constitutional issues: no complaint that American rights were violated; no claim that Parliament lacked authority to levy such duties. They addressed only economic considerations, consistently treating the Sugar Act as a regulation of trade. The British used this lack of objection to argue that the Americans accepted the authority of Parliament to impose port duties. "The Amount of the Impositions has been complained of; the Policy of the Laws has been objected to; *but the Right of making such a Law, has never been questioned.*"[21]

James Otis (in a famous essay of 1764 that we will see in chapter 6) explained the American attitude.

The act of the 6th of his late Majesty, though it imposes a *duty* in terms, has been said to be designed for a *prohibition*, which is probable from the sums imposed; and 'tis pity it had not been so expressed, as there is *not the least doubt of the just and equitable right of the Parliament* to lay prohibitions through the dominions when they think the good of the whole requires it.[22]

British philosopher and pamphleteer Richard Price (more than a decade after Otis) was specific about the American response.

In this act, the duties imposed are said to be given and granted by the Parliament to the King; and this is the first American act in which these words have been used. But notwithstanding this, as the act had the appearance of being only a regulation of trade, the colonies submitted to it.[23]

There was, however, some recognition that the act might be a precedent for later taxation. Thomas Cushing wrote Jasper Mauduit late in January 1764.

The Generall Court have mett and have chose a large Committee of both Houses to consider how our Trade is affected by the Act of Parliament laying a duty upon Molasses, etc. The Committee have mett and we are preparing Instructions for you upon this matter. I find the Committee in general are of opinion that this Act is at this time put in rigorous execution *in order to obtain our Consent to some Dutys being laid*, but this is look'd upon of dangerous consequence as it will be conceeding to the Parliaments having a Right to Tax our trade which we can't by any means think of admitting, as it would be *contrary to a fundamentall Principall of our Constitution vizt. That all Taxes ought to originate with the people.*[24]

Cushing wrote Mauduit again on February 11, informing him that the instructions were completed and being sent to him forthwith. The instructions did not reach Mauduit in time to influence the renewal of the Sugar Act. The timing of events in London and Boston is part of the story. At this point, Mauduit had already written that renewal of the Sugar Act of 1733 was underway. In his letter of December 30, 1763—the letter being in transit in early February 1764—he explained about reduction of the molasses duty.

This scheme is resumed, and the quantum of the duty is to be one of the first things considered immediately of the meeting of the parliament. All agree that a practicable duty should be laid, and the payment of it enforced. To attempt to controvert either of these would be to no manner of purpose.[25]

So the instructions to oppose the duties on a constitutional basis were on the way to Mauduit at the same time the letter reporting the futility of such opposition was on its way to Massachusetts.

In understanding the evolution in thinking of American popular leaders, an important factor is that these documents were created early in the year—before the British passed the Sugar Act of 1764 and revealed the plan to implement stamp duties. "In the overall development of the Revolutionary movement, these statements of colonial opinion, written before the passage of the Sugar Act, are of considerable importance."

> For not only do they express the colonists' objections to the economic reorganization of the empire, but they mark the last point at which objections to Parliamentary action affecting them could generally be voiced without reference to ideology. The most striking fact about these addresses and petitions is their entire devotion to economic arguments: nowhere do they appeal to constitutional issues; nowhere was Parliament's right to pass such laws officially questioned.[26]

In early 1764, it was easy enough for the Americans to think that assertions about enforcement of the laws of trade and the importance of revenue were simply a repeat of the rote recitations of years past— that the British pronouncements were merely a continuation of the same-old, same-old jawboning from the ministry. As a consequence, these protests were mild, thoroughly accepting the idea of control of trade by Great Britain, expecting the American grievance about the economic burden to be taken seriously by the mother country, and trusting that the colonies would not be economically harmed. The mild nature of the protests reflects that the Americans could not see that the British plans so far revealed were merely the first step in a policy change that was soon to be considered a manifest violation of their just and long-enjoyed rights.

PART TWO

Taxation

We will deal with two forms of taxation in 1764. At the end of chapter 1, we saw Richard Jackson mention customs duties, or port duties, what came to be known as *external* taxes. Since "the mother country may prohibit foreign Trade, it may therefore tax it." He continues, "but I dread *internal* taxes." An internal tax—or inland tax, or excise tax—is exactly what is soon to be planned by Parliament, and judged by the Americans to be unprecedented and unconstitutional.

Massachusetts lieutenant governor Thomas Hutchinson, on July 23, 1764, wrote a letter to Jackson in which he expressed his opinion that there was no effective difference between customs duties and an internal tax.

How are the Privileges of the People less affected [by the payment of duties] than by an internal tax? Is it any difference to me whether I pay three pounds ten shillings duty for a Pipe of wine to an officer of Impost or whether I pay the same sum by an excise of nine pence per Gallon to an excise Officer?[1]

Chapter 3 tells three stories. First, Prime Minister Grenville puts forth the rationale for the use of customs duties to produce revenue: an external tax. Second, he asserts the need for stamp duties in America, and asserts the right of Parliament to impose that internal tax. The third story is a brief description of the Sugar Act (the renewal of the Molasses Act), and an analysis of its general nature.[2]

Chapter 4 is straightforward: notice to America that stamp duties will be imposed in the next session of Parliament. The informal American response is immediate: warnings that the stamp duties will be unproductive and unpopular. The more formal response, the stance taken by each colony, sits fomenting in the background.

Three

The Sugar Act

PARLIAMENT OPENED IN NOVEMBER 1763. THE KING'S SPEECH called for attention to "the heavy debts contracted in the course of the late war." He called for both frugality and "the improvement of the public revenue, by such regulations as shall be judged most expedient for that purpose."[1] Discussion about America was put aside for a few months to deal with pressing local matters, but on March 7, 1764, George Grenville, in his role as chancellor of the exchequer, informed the House that in two days he would introduce the budget, "particularly as to the taxing America." The topic was not without controversy. "William Beckford at once raised what would become the central issue of the Stamp Act Crisis, the constitutional role in this respect of 'the American legislatures.'"[2] (The role being referred to is the taxation authority previously granted to the legislature of each colony.)

PASSAGE OF THE ACT

March 9, 1764, is a day of considerable importance to the history of the American Revolution.

In the House of Commons:
The Order of the Day being read, for the House to resolve itself

into a Committee of the whole House, to consider further of Ways
and Means for raising the Supply granted to his Majesty.

This is the day the British more or less officially unveiled the policy change that had been brewing for over a year. Grenville presented
to the Committee on Ways and Means his budget for the improvement of the public revenue. He included a set of resolutions that were
the basis for duties of the Sugar Act of 1764 (the renewal of the Molasses Act so strongly protested by the Americans) and—since the
new duties were not expected to raise adequate revenue—he included
a resolution stating the need for an additional tax: stamp duties.

After a long general introduction, including mention of Britain's
"great debt" and that one solution is "to collect the Customs and
prevent abuses by lowering the rate," he declares that since they now
are at peace, "let us make the best use of it." (The following account
of Grenville's presentation and the subsequent debate is not a tran-
script of the proceedings but rather a report of what occurred.)[3]

> The House comes to the resolution *to raise the revenue in America*
> for defending itself. We have expended much in America. Let us now
> avail ourselves of the fruits of that expense. The *great object to rec-
> oncile* the regulation of commerce with an increase of revenue.

It is exactly this attempt to reconcile regulation and revenue that
conflates the two issues in a manner that obscures the intent of the
Sugar Act.

> With this view particularly desirable to prevent intercourse of
> America with foreign nations. And yet many colonies have such a
> trade. Such a trade has been opened by three or four colonies with
> France to the amount of £4 or 500,000 a year.
> Great attention given to prevent this practice by giving direc-
> tions to the commissioners to prevent smuggling. This has been
> attended with success, the proportion from England has increased.

"But this is not enough; you must collect the revenue from the
plantations." He states the rationale for a preferential tariff.

First object would be to permit West Indian trade, at the same time to regulate the other. To allow certain commodities from the French islands which are absolutely necessary, but to give preference to our own colonies' manufactures by paying duty upon the others.

He describes the new molasses duty.

A duty of 6d. per gallon upon molasses by the 6th of the late King was too heavy; this duty to be lowered therefore to 3d. But the quantity so doubtful that he cannot form any certain estimate; perhaps £40, 50 or 60,000.

Why threepence duty? Grenville had calculated that level of duty as the value that would maximize revenue. He believed it to be an imposition the Americans would accept as reasonable; that merchants would import duty-paid molasses in preference to smuggling.

He brings up the need for additional regulation of trade and addresses the "difficulty of executing these regulations." Here is the problem: it is "difficult to find good officers who will go to North America."

Smuggling therefore will continue and therefore, as this will diminish the revenue, some *further tax will be necessary* to defray the expense of North America.

He introduces the topic that will dominate the next two years of the relationship between Great Britain and America.

Stamp duties the least exceptionable because it requires few officers and even collects itself. The only danger is forgery.

The related resolve is to become the focus of American protest for the remainder of the year—the soon-to-be-controversial and eventually infamous fifteenth resolution (of twenty-four he introduced that day, all others dealing with the Sugar Act).

That, towards further defraying the said Expences, it may be proper to charge certain Stamp Duties in the said Colonies and Plantations.

Although there had been hints throughout 1763 and early 1764 that the British policy had turned toward a focus on extracting revenue from the colonies in North America, this simple resolve seals the deal.

At this point, having heard rumblings to the contrary, Grenville wishes to affirm that Parliament holds the authority to impose such a tax on America. This next statement and the following discussion are highly significant as an indication of the mood and intent of Parliament.

He is convinced this country have the right to impose an inland tax. . . . If any man doubts the right of this country he will take the opinion of the committee immediately.

No man doubted. (One colonial agent reported that "the Members interested in the Plantations expressed great surprise that a doubt of that nature could ever exist.") As part of his discussion, Grenville emphasized that "Britain has an inherent right to lay inland duties there." His most dramatic statement was that "the very sovereignty of this kingdom depends on it." This phrase establishes a framework for British perception of the later American protests: to deny the right of Parliament to levy such a tax is denial of the supremacy of Parliament, denial of *the very sovereignty of this kingdom*.

The resolution to levy stamp duties, and the unanimous consent to the right of Britain to levy such an inland tax on the colonies, laid the groundwork for what would eventually become known as the Stamp Act Crisis.[4] The Americans understood the fifteenth resolution to be both an assertion of the right of Parliament to tax the colonies and a declaration that Parliament intended to exercise that right.

Grenville begins to close. "He owns the officers of the revenue must strike in the dark. However, he thinks this the best plan." As his final words he makes an obscure statement that hints at a possible alternative to the imposition of internal taxes by Parliament. "He would likewise wish to follow to a certain degree the inclination of the people in North America if they will agree to the end."

First to rise was Sir William Baker. He agreed "perfectly to our right to tax the colonies." (But he thought the tax should be twopence at first, then raised later.)

Charles Jenkinson followed Baker. "He could easily confirm the right of England to impose taxes upon North America from Acts of Parliament and resolutions of the House of Commons."

John Huske, a native of New Hampshire who had resided in England for twenty-five years, had much to say. (He sometimes speaks as a British legislator, sometimes as an American.)

> Our laws have created smuggling even by force. Smugglers of molasses instead of being infamous are called patriots in North America. Nothing but a low duty can prevent it.

He makes an important assertion, especially coming from one knowledgeable about America. "No doubt can exist of the right to tax North America in England. We [Americans] know we are subject to the legislature of this country." (Generally considered a friend of America, he is later much criticized for this admission.)

But he objects to the timing of the stamp duties.

> Notice ought to be sent to North America of any important business which relates to them. . . . North American agents are always desired to play for time if anything occurs in Parliament which materially affects their interest.

"Would have this law read two times, printed and then sent to America for their opinion about it." He provides a small tutorial on molasses, the level of duty, and smuggling.

> Molasses duty has never brought in anything. French King has lately given our ships leave to take the molasses from his islands, which diminishes the expense per gallon of it, and therefore he approves of a duty of 2d. which he thinks much better than 3d., as there will be less temptation to smuggling. The molasses are

bought off foreigners by the superfluous lumber of our province and other things.

He elaborates on smuggling. "30 ships go from New England every year laden with nothing but rum, and bring back gold dust, elephants' teeth and slaves for the sugar planters." He repeats the standard colonial argument that "the more North America gets, the more it will be able to remit to us for manufactures." Then he provides a negative analysis of the threepence duty.

A duty on molasses at 2d per gallon will yield about £58,000; at 3d it will not produce £25,000. If you keep the duty on molasses so high as to discourage it, you will lead the Americans into the corn distillery which will hurt the country gentlemen here.

William Beckford supported customs duties; he asserted "the colonies should be subservient to the mother country, which should be the monopolizer." Although he did not again raise the role of the American legislatures as he did on March 7, he was the only member who was noted as being "against the stamp duties."

Grenville spoke again. "As to stamp duty, desired it might be done with good will. That for the present session it might go no farther than a resolution." It is not clear from context, or from later claims over the years, whether Grenville had always intended to postpone the stamp duties until 1765, or if it was objections by Huske and others that caused him to postpone. The postponement is important to the story of 1764 since it allowed time for American objections to be expressed during the year, raising constitutional arguments against the stamp duty even before the Stamp Act was passed in 1765.[5]

Although there was modest discussion regarding the level of duty, there was no opposition to the bill. And there was no attempt to present American objections. The debate ended quietly. "Thus with much temper and great attention to what Mr. Grenville said, ended this important day at about half hour past nine."

The Committee on Ways and Means submitted twenty-four resolutions to the full House; most were approved on March 10. Here are the resolutions of greatest importance to the story of 1764.

Molasses duty:

[12] Resolved, That it is the Opinion of this Committee, That from and after the said 29th Day of September 1764, in lieu of the Duty granted by the said Act [i.e., the act of 1733] upon Molasses and Syrups, a Duty of Threepence Sterling Money per Gallon, be laid upon all Molasses and Syrups, of the Growth, Product, or Manufacture, of any foreign American Colony or Plantation, imported into the British Colonies and Plantations in America.

Resolution 13 set the duties for sugar, and resolution 14 established that the "Produce of all the Said Duties" shall be reserved for "defraying the necessary Expences of defending, protecting, and securing, the British colonies and plantations in America."
Stamp duties:

[15] Resolved, That it is the Opinion of this Committee, That, towards further defraying the said Expences, it may be proper to charge certain Stamp Duties in the said Colonies and Plantations.

Resolution 20 prohibited the importation of foreign rum or spirits from the West Indies.

On March 12, the House ordered that the bill was to include regulations necessary for its enforcement: specifically, "for more effectually preventing the clandestine Exportation, Importation, and Conveyance of Goods to and from the British Colonies and Plantations in America." This order resulted in clauses of the act dictating extensive procedures tightening up the regulation of trade.

The resulting bill was approved by the Commons on March 30, sent up to the Lords, and passed (without debate) on April 4. It received the royal assent on April 5, 1764. The King's Speech, when he closed the session of Parliament on April 19, included these words of praise for the House of Commons.

The wise regulations which have been established to augment the public revenues, to unite the interests of the most distant possessions of my crown, and to encourage and secure their commerce with Great Britain, call for my hearty approbation.[6]

THE SUGAR ACT

The Sugar Act (4 George III c. 15) was the renewal (and amendment) of the Molasses Act, the Sugar Act of 1733. This renewal was exactly the British action feared and protested against by the American petitions and essays of early 1764 (chapter 2). At first look, the Sugar Act seemed to be nothing more than a renewal. That apparently straightforward appearance helped lead the Americans to a belief that the Sugar Act was a regulation of trade, just like the act of 1733. However, from a modern point of view, the amendments are so far-reaching that it is best thought of as a *replacement* for the earlier act. Indeed, its intent was, "in the first place to raise a colonial revenue, and in the second to reform the old colonial system, both in its administrative and in its economic features. It was the first statute distinctly taxing the colonies, and marked a radically new departure in colonial policy."[7] It is even fair to say that the Sugar Act of 1764 "was the first unmistakable proof to the colonists that the Grenville administration had seriously undertaken the revision of existing relationships between England and America."[8]

The title.

> An act for granting certain duties in the British colonies and plantations in America; for *continuing, amending, and making perpetual* [the Molasses Act]; for applying the produce of such duties . . . towards defraying the expences of defending, protecting, and securing the said colonies and plantations . . . and more effectually preventing the clandestine conveyance of goods to and from the said colonies and plantations, and *improving and securing the trade* between the same and Great Britain.[9]

The act grants duties, but is also trade regulation: *improving and securing the trade.* The preamble is more direct about raising revenue.

The preamble.

> Whereas it is expedient that new provisions and regulations should be established for *improving the revenue* of this kingdom, and for extending and securing the navigation and commerce be-

tween Great Britain and your Majesty's dominions in America,
which, by the peace, have been so happily enlarged; and whereas
it is *just and necessary that a revenue be raised*, in your Majesty's
said dominions in America, for defraying the expenses of defending, protecting, and securing the same; we, your Majesty's most
dutiful and loyal subjects, the commons of Great Britain, in parliament assembled, being desirous to make some provision, in this
present session of parliament, towards raising the said revenue in
America, have *resolved to give and grant unto your Majesty* the
several rates and duties herein after-mentioned.

We see an important phrase that denotes a money bill: "that a revenue be raised." And we see the "give and grant" words of donation.
The Molasses Act also used words of donation, but this is the first
act dealing with America that contains both these phrases strongly
characteristic of taxation.

After September 29, 1764, "there shall be raised, levied, collected,
and paid . . . the several rates and duties following; that is to say,"

For every hundred weight avoirdupois of such foreign white or
clayed sugars, one pound two shillings, over and above all other
duties imposed by any former act of parliament [hence one pound
seven shillings total]
For every pound weight avoirdupois of such foreign indigo, six pence
For every hundred weight avoirdupois of such foreign coffee,
which shall be imported from any place, except Great Britain, two
pounds, nineteen shillings, and nine pence
For every ton of wine [imported directly from the Madeira islands]
. . . the sum of seven pounds

The same ton of Madeira wine imported via Great Britain would
bear a duty of only ten shillings. (The same as other wine imported
from Great Britain.)

[Many duties on] silks, bengals . . . callico . . . foreign linen cloth . . .
For every hundred weight avoirdupois of such British coffee, seven
shillings

For every pound weight avoirdupois of such British pimento, one
halfpenny

A later clause prohibits the importation of foreign rum from the
West Indies.

In clause V, the new act is decreed to be effective from September
29, 1764, and the act of 1733, "is hereby made perpetual."

A crucial alteration is the reduction in the molasses duty, intended
to partly meet the American desires expressed in early 1764.

VI. In lieu and instead of the rate and duty imposed by the said
act upon molasses and syrups, there shall . . . be raised, levied,
collected, and paid, unto his Majesty, his heirs and successors, for
and upon every gallon of molasses or syrups, being the growth,
product, or manufacture, of any colony or plantation in America,
not under the dominion of his Majesty, his heir or successors,
which shall be imported or brought into any colony or plantation
in America, which now is, or hereafter may be, under the dominion of his Majesty, his heirs or successors, *the sum of three pence.*

Here is the clause that nails down the purpose of the act for support of the army in America.

XI. And it is hereby further enacted . . . that all the monies . . . shall
be paid into the receipt of his Majesty's Exchequer, and shall be entered separate and apart from all other monies paid . . . and shall be
there reserved to be, from time to time, disposed of by parliament,
towards defraying the necessary expences of defending, protecting,
and securing, the British colonies and plantations in America.

The intent of this requirement is that the monies received be used
exclusively in America. This is important since the duties were to be
collected in sterling money (as in the Molasses Act). Some Americans
protested that the act would remove hard currency from America.
This was incorrect. (But it was true, and a grievance, that duties collected in the established colonies would generally be expended in the
recently acquired territory, or on the frontier.)

The act contains additional clauses, forty-seven in total, defining regulatory processes and procedures intended to provide the foundation for strict enforcement of customs regulations. Americans began to find the regulations burdensome, and complained in 1764, but with one exception they played no major role in the controversy that year. The following clause provides for prosecution in courts of admiralty, courts in which there is no jury. The judge rules not only on matters of law but also on matters of fact—the role of juries in common-law courts.

> XLI. All the forfeitures and penalties *inflicted by this or any other act or acts of parliament relating to the trade and revenues* of the said British colonies or plantations in America, which shall be incurred there, shall and may be prosecuted, sued for, and recovered in any court of record, or in any court of admiralty . . . at the election of the informer or prosecutor.

The Americans protested this clause as an inappropriate extension of the role of admiralty courts, and as unconstitutional, a violation of the right to trial by jury.[10]

I am skipping the clauses about restrictions but do not want to downplay the adverse effect of those procedures combined with strict enforcement. Here is a complaint from William Allen, the chief justice of Pennsylvania, writing from Philadelphia to Barclay & Sons in London on November 20.

> No doubt you will hear fully of the low Ebb of Trade, which is distressed exceedingly; even the Intercourse between here & New Jersey is, in a great Measure interrupted, which was carried on in Flats & small Boats, and the Produce of the Western part of that Colony shipped oft from this City, But now, one of those poor fellows cannot take in a few Staves, or Pig Iron, or Bar Iron, or Tar &c, but they must go thirty or forty Miles, or more to give Bond, the Charge of which & his travelling, make the Burthen intolerable.
>
> It never was the Intention of the Legislature at home to destroy this little River-Trade, which is carried on in a kind of Market

Boats, but their Emulations were only for Sea Vessels. This is a general Complaint all over the Continent; Such Measures will soon make us poor, but our Creditors in England will suffer with us. We must learn Frugality and make all our necessaries ourselves, for we shall soon not be able to get them any other way, as our Money is gone, and our Credit will soon be at an end.[11]

THE CURRENCY ACT

Following on the heels of the Sugar Act, Parliament passed "An Act to prevent paper bills of credit . . . from being declared to be a legal tender in payments of money." It is often called the Currency Act. The lack of specie—a constant problem in the colonies—brought about the need for colonial paper currency to circulate, and be proclaimed legal tender, in order to simplify trade. Although it was a grievance—the Americans lobbying against its enactment and protesting afterward—it was a significantly smaller issue than taxation.

REPORTS FROM THE MAUDUITS

On March 13, Massachusetts agent Jasper Mauduit forwarded a copy of the resolutions along with this information about the Grenville discussion on March 9.

The Stamp duty you will see is deferr'd till next year. I mean the actual laying it. Mr. Grenville being willing to give the Provinces their option to *raise that or some equivalent tax.* Desirous as he express'd himself to consult the Ease, the Quiet, and the Goodwill of the Colonies.[12]

What I characterized as an obscure statement by Grenville ("wish to follow to a certain degree the inclination of the people in North America") was not so obscure to Mauduit. He believed, and he was not the only agent to so believe, that Grenville was open to an alternative source of revenue. The agents will pursue that issue in May (chapter 4).

On April 7, Mauduit provided a copy of the Sugar Act.

The present sense of Parliament is such that I should only flatter and deceive the General Court if I led them to imagine that any one Man of Consequence there would stand up in his place and avow an opinion that America ought not to bear at least the greater part of the expense of its own Government.[13]

Israel Mauduit wrote on the same day.

There did not seem to be a single man in Parliament who thought that the conquered provinces ought to be left without Troops, or that England after having run so deeply in Debt for the conquering of these provinces, by which Stability & Security is given to all the American Governments, should now tax itself for the maintenance of them.[14]

FIRST NEWS ARRIVES IN AMERICA

On May 10, 1764, the first widespread, reliable news of the Sugar Act was published in the *Pennsylvania Gazette* and quickly promulgated throughout the colonies.

Our other Advices by the Packet are, that a Scheme of Taxation of the American Colonies has for some Time been in Agitation: That it had been *previously debated* in Parliament, whether they had Power to lay such a Tax on Colonies which had no Representatives in Parliament, and determined in the Affirmative.

That on the Ninth of March, Mr. [Grenville] made a long Harrangue on the melancholy State of the Nation, overloaded with heavy Taxes, and a Debt of £146 Millions, £52 Millions of which had arisen in the four last Years: That by a Computation, which he laid before the House, £360,000 Sterling per Annum was expended on North-America, and therefore it was but reasonable they should support the Troops sent out for their Defence, and all the other particular Expence of the Nation on their Account.

The news was specific about several of the proposed duties, including "a Duty of 3d. per Gallon on foreign Melasses."

Besides this, an internal Tax was proposed, a Stamp Duty, &c.
but many Members warmly opposing it, this was deferred till next
Session; but it was feared that the Tax upon foreign Goods would
pass into a Law this Session. That these Colonies are under great
Disadvantages, in not having sufficient Interest in Parliament;
from the Want of which, the West Indies have been able to carry
any Point against them.[15]

THE NATURE OF THE SUGAR ACT

Well, what was the act aimed at? Regulating trade? Raising revenue?
Thomas Whately (a secretary to the Lords of the Treasury and a
particularly close confidant of and spokesman for Grenville) provided in January 1765 a lengthy justification for the Sugar Act. He
highlights the mixture of revenue and trade regulation.

[The] several Duties imposed by Parliament . . . appear to have
been judiciously chosen, not only with a View to the Revenue,
which they will produce; but for other, and in my Opinion, greater
political Purposes; [including enhancing] the Trade of Great
Britain, and to the Connection between her and her Colonies.

On balance, the greater purpose seems to give the nod to trade
regulation.

In other Countries Custom-house Duties are for the most Part, little more than a Branch of the Revenue: In the Colonies they are a
political Regulation, and enforce the Observance of those wise
Laws to which the great Increase of our Trade and naval Power
are principally owing. The Aim of those Laws is to confine the
European Commerce of the Colonies to the Mother Country: to
provide that their most valuable Commodities shall be exported
either to Great Britain or to British Plantations; and to secure the
Navigation of all American Exports and Imports to British Ships
and British Subjects only.[16]

But the Sugar Act was an act of revenue, no doubt about it. However foggy the terrain in 1764, later events proved it to be a tax. The

key distinction between the Sugar Act and all previous acts that imposed duties on imports is that it was genuinely enacted for—and stated as having the purpose of—raising revenue. No earlier American act, including the ambiguous Molasses Act, was intended to collect duties on imports for the purpose of revenue.

The First Continental Congress had no question about its purpose. This resolve on October 14, 1774, specifically identifies the Sugar Act. "The several acts of 4 Geo. III. ch. 15, and [later acts] . . . which impose duties *for the purpose of raising a revenue in America* . . . are subversive of American rights."[17]

THE SUGAR ACT AND COLONIAL POLICY

Now that we have seen the Sugar Act, it is time to look at a powerful later statement about its relation to the implementation of the new colonial policy. Edmund Burke addressed the issue in the House of Commons on April 19, 1774 (in his famous Speech on American Taxation).

In that speech, he scolds the House for its change in colonial policy. "No act avowedly for the purpose of revenue" is found in the statute book until 1764. "All before this period stood on commercial regulation and restraint." He elaborates.

> Whether you were right or wrong in establishing the Colonies on the principles of commercial monopoly, rather than on that of revenue, is at this day a problem of mere speculation. *You cannot have both by the same authority.* To join together the restraints of an universal internal and external monopoly, with an universal internal and external taxation, is an unnatural union; perfect uncompensated slavery.

He pinpoints the Sugar Act as marking the beginning of a new policy.

> The grand manoeuvre in that business of new regulating the colonies, was the 15th act of the fourth of George 3; which . . . opened *a new principle: and here properly began the second period of the policy of this country with regard to the colonies;* by

which the scheme of a regular plantation parliamentary revenue
was adopted in theory, and settled in practice. A revenue not substituted in the place of, but superadded to, a monopoly; which
monopoly was enforced at the same time with additional strict-
ness, and the execution put into military hands.

The act was full of assertions of taxation.

This act, Sir, had for the first time the title of "granting duties in
the colonies and plantations of America;" and for the first time it
was asserted in the preamble, "that it was just and necessary that
a revenue should be raised there." Then came the technical words
of "giving and granting;" and thus a complete American Revenue
Act was made in all the forms, and with a full avowal of the right,
equity, policy, and even necessity of taxing the colonies, without
any formal consent of theirs.

He points out good reason for the Americans to be concerned
about the future.

There are contained also in the preamble to that Act these very
remarkable words—the Commons, &c.— "being desirous to
make some provision in the present session of Parliament towards
raising the said revenue." *By these words it appeared to the
colonies that this act was but a beginning of sorrows*; that every
session was to produce something of the same kind; that we were
to go on from day to day, in charging them with such taxes as we
pleased, for such a military force as we should think proper.

He later refers to lack of objection to the Sugar Act.

When the first American Revenue Act (the Act in 1764, imposing
the port duties) passed, the Americans did not object to the principle.

And provides the reason. "The duties were port duties, *like those
they had been accustomed to bear.*"[18]

The planned stamp duties are *internal* taxation. In contrast, the Sugar Act levies customs duties: *external* taxation. It makes sense now to elaborate on the distinction between the two. It is difficult to pin down external taxation; in fact, it is impossible to provide a coherent definition: different spokesmen used it in different ways, rarely with an explanation. In fact, external tax is often used as a synonym for customs duty or port duty (the levy of which Americans acknowledged as being within the rightful authority of Parliament). So, in many contexts, an external tax is not a tax. We need some clarification.

The best explanation of how the British came to their understanding of the American position on internal and external taxation is the testimony given by Benjamin Franklin to the House of Commons in February 1766 (in the format of a stylized question-and-answer session). His answers were uniquely authoritative in creating the British understanding (perhaps misunderstanding) of the American position on this issue. (This is from the same question-and-answer session before the House of Commons that I presented in the introduction to this book.)

In the following segment, he provides rationale for the lack of American protest to external taxes in 1764 and 1765.

Q. Did you ever hear the authority of parliament to make laws for America questioned till lately?

A. The authority of parliament was allowed to be valid in all laws, except such as should lay internal taxes. It was never disputed in laying duties to regulate commerce.

He is asked another question on the same topic.

Q. You say the Colonies have always submitted to external taxes, and object to the right of parliament only in laying internal taxes; now can you shew that there is any kind of difference between the two taxes to the Colony on which they may be laid?

Here is a straightforward definition of an external tax.

A. I think the difference is very great. *An external tax is a duty
laid on commodities imported*; that duty is added to the first cost,
and other charges on the commodity, and when it is offered to
sale, makes a part of the price. If the people do not like it at that
price, they refuse it; they are not obliged to pay it. But an internal
tax is forced from the people without their consent, if not laid by
their own representatives.

And a similar question, after Franklin has discussed internal (excise) taxes:

Q. You say [Americans] do not object to the right of parliament,
in laying duties on goods to be paid on their importation; now, is
there any kind of difference between a duty on the importation of
goods and an excise on their consumption?

A. Yes; a very material one; an excise, for the reasons I just mentioned, they think you can have no right to lay within their country. But the sea is yours; you maintain, by your fleets, the safety
of navigation in it, and keep it clear of pirates; you may have
therefore a natural and equitable right to some toll or duty on
merchandizes carried through that part of your dominions, towards defraying the expence you are at in ships to maintain the
safety of that carriage.

In answer to yet another question, Franklin characterized the
American idea of internal and external taxes: "By taxes they mean
internal taxes; by duties they mean customs; these are the ideas of
the language."[19] An alternate source quotes Franklin slightly differently. "By the word taxes they have always considered internal taxes
only, and when they mean external taxes they use the word duties."[20]
(The question-and-answer session was later published as *The Examination of Doctor Benjamin Franklin, before an August Assembly*.)
Eventually, the unified American stance was to reject all forms of
taxation (while accepting trade regulation). The First Continental

Congress in 1764 took the position, "We cheerfully consent to the operation of such acts of the British parliament, as are bonfide, restrained to the regulation of our external commerce . . . excluding every idea of taxation, *internal or external*, for raising a revenue on the subjects in America without their consent."[21]

Four

Notification of
Stamp Duties

ONTHS AFTER THE ASSERTION THAT "IT MAY BE PROPER TO charge certain Stamp Duties," and despite the lack of precision regarding the postponement (rationale or timing), Grenville had offered no additional information.

AMERICANS SEEK INFORMATION

In May, the colonial agents felt they needed specific information about Grenville's plans, including his willingness to allow the option of some equivalent tax as an alternative to stamp duties. They requested a meeting with him, which he granted for May 17, 1764. On May 26, Jasper Mauduit wrote Massachusetts, reporting secondhand from his brother Israel, who attended the meeting. "A few days ago, several of the Agents waited upon Mr. Grenville to know his intentions upon that subject [stamp duties]." Grenville made this point.

> That of the several Inland Duties, that of the stamps was the most equal, required the fewest officers, and was attended with least Expense in the Collecting of it. That therefore, tho he doubted not but that the Colonies would wish rather to have no tax at all; yet

as the necessities of Government rendered it an indispensable duty, he should certainly bring in such a Bill. And in the meantime he should leave it to each province to *signify their Assent to such a Bill in General, or their requests about any particular modifications of it as they should think fit.*

Grenville essentially affirmed that Parliament would, in fact, levy stamp duties. Israel Mauduit then asked about specifics of the bill.

My Brother took the Liberty of desiring to have the particular heads of the Bill; without which he said it would be asking the province to assent to they did not know what. But was answered, that that was not necessary. That everyone knew the stamp laws here; and that this Bill is intended to be formed upon the same plan.[1]

Little new was revealed and nothing resolved, but several agents reported in such a manner as to suggest that Grenville would, in fact, take into account alternatives to the stamp duties. A few colonies made fits and starts at taking advantage of an apparent opportunity but did nothing that affected the main stream of protest.

OFFICIAL NOTIFICATION

Even four months after his fifteenth resolution, Grenville had not yet officially notified the colonial governors of his intent to levy stamp duties. Charles Jenkinson, a secretary to the Lords of the Treasury, wrote Grenville on July 2, 1764, prompting him to take some official action.

In the last session of Parliament, you assigned as a reason for not going on with the Stamp Act, that you waited only for further information on that subject. This having been said, *should not Government appear to take some step for that purpose?* I mentioned this to you soon after the Parliament was up. I remember your objections to it; but I think the information may be procured in a manner to obviate those objections, and without it we may perhaps be accused of neglect.[2]

Six weeks later, Secretary of State Halifax sent this circular letter to colonial governors, making official notification of Grenville's plan.

August 11, 1764
Sir,
The House of Commons having, in the last Session of Parliament,
come to a Resolution, it is His Majesty's Pleasure, that you should
transmit to me, without Delay, a List of all Instruments made Use
of in publick Transactions, Law Proceedings, Grants, Con-
veyances, Securities of Land or Money, within Your Government,
with proper &sufficient Descriptions of the same, in Order that
if Parliament should think proper to pursue the Intention of the
aforesaid Resolution, they may thereby be enabled to carry it into
Execution, in the most effectual and least burthensome Manner.[3]

Americans correctly took this (despite the hedge, "if Parliament
should think proper") as official notification that the duties would
be imposed. The governors responded as requested, but even the earliest responses did not arrive in London until December and hence
had little effect on the statute. I'll provide one example of a response.

Connecticut governor Thomas Fitch sent the list of requested documents to Halifax on November 13. Fitch took the opportunity to
politely object to the entire idea of the stamp duty.

It will appear by this List that the public Instruments can be
Charged with no Burden but what must Lye immediately on the
Colony Treasury already Exhausted by the War. . . . The People
in General are also so involved that new Burdens will not only be
Distressing but greatly Discouraging in their Struggles to Extricate
themselves from their Debts incurred during the Late War. Suffer
me my Lord to Intreat on their Behalf that they may be Excused
from this new Duty which appears to them so grievous.[4]

This letter did not reach London until January 16, 1765. Here are
some of the documents Fitch provided:

A commission to the chief judge of the Superior Court (and other
judges)
A commission to a colonel, lieutenant colonel, and major of each
regiment

Writs: both summonses and attachments, which include the writ
Subpoena for witnesses
Petitions and memorials to the General Assembly
Deeds of conveyance of lands and mortgage deeds of lands
Bonds for security of money
Wills

In addition to the letter from Halifax, there were also quasi-official notifications, such as Thomas Whately writing a British official in America on August 14, 1764. In establishing his purpose for writing, he remarked, "I mean ye stamp duty, which unless unforeseen objections occur will probably be extended next year to America."[5]

UNOFFICIAL NOTIFICATION

Even earlier than the official notification, after Whately in spring 1764 was assigned responsibility to prepare the Stamp Act, he sought information from his correspondents in America. Two letters in response to Whately's requests are of particular importance, offering observations and grievances about the Sugar Act and the planned Stamp Act.

Jared Ingersoll

In June, Whately wrote his Connecticut friend Jared Ingersoll (an important lawyer and influential statesman) to acquaint him with the plans of the ministry and to ask him some questions about how to structure the stamp duties.

> Mr. Grenville's favour has made me Secretary to the Treasury; a Place of too much Business to be compatible with any other. I have therefore quitted the Bar & am now immers'd in Politics, Parliament, and Revenue. . . . I often see our friend Jackson & from him have frequently heard of your Welfare. His Knowledge in American Affairs is of public Use when America is become so much the Object of the Attention of the Ministry. Many Regulations both with regard to its Settlement & its Revenue have already been made by this time.
>
> I suppose you are apprized of them & you would oblige me greatly by informing me of the Reception they meet with in your

part of the World, & much more by communicating to me your own free Sentiments upon them. I should be happy to know the genuine Opinion of sensible Men in the Colonies upon Subjects equally interesting both to them & to us.

Whately himself, and no doubt indicative of the attitude of Grenville, is genuinely concerned with the welfare of the colonies.

You know I always from Inclination interested myself in their Prosperity. My present Situation necessarily employs me often in their Affairs & I therefore am anxious to get all the Information I can in relation to them. All new Taxes are open to Examination; & I should be glad to know what you & your people think of those that have been imposed this Session. Their produce is doubt-ful; perhaps you may make a Guess at it so far as your province is concern'd; but *certainly these will not be sufficient to defray that Share of ye American Expence* which America ought & is able to bear. Others must be added. What they will be will in some degree depend on the Accounts which will be received from thence.

Whately provides some rationale for postponement of the stamp duties, clarifying the intent to gain information, but also adding mud to the water.

A Stamp Act has been proposed. Its produce would be great as is generally supposed here, from ye great Number of Law Suits in most of ye Colonies, but it was not carried into Execution, *out of tenderness to them & to give them time to furnish ye necessary Information for this, or to suggest any better Mode of Taxation.*

Tenderness to the Americans? Whately has no clue that the details of *how* to tax will be overwhelmed by the very *idea* of the levy of a stamp tax by Parliament. Whately gets to specific questions.

Would it yield a considerable Revenue if the Duty were low upon mercantile Instruments, high upon gratuitous Grants of Lands, and moderate upon Law Proceedings? Would ye Execution of such a Law be attended with great Inconveniencies, or open to frequent Evasions which could not be guarded against? At least, it must be allow'd to be as general an Imposition as can be devised & in that respect seems preferable to a Tax upon Negroes, which would affect ye Southern much more than ye Northern Colonies, tho' that on the other hand would be more easily collected & less liable to Evasion.

If either of these would be very exceptionable can you suggest any other? You will highly oblige me by furnishing me with any Information relative to ye Revenue, to the Regulations necessary against Smuggling & the Effect of those already made, & to any other point that concerns the Colonies. I am anxious on the Subject myself & I can find Opportunities to make good Use of any Information I receive. My Earnestness about it has you see hurried me into a long Letter.[6]

His need to ask these questions, showing his lack of understanding of the likely response to such taxation, is indicative of a naïve attitude in the ministry.

Ingersoll received the letter on July 4, responding on July 6. His letter is a warning to Great Britain that things will not go well. "You Desire my opinion upon the late Act of trade & upon the proposed taxations which respect America." He has a lot to say, starting with the recent Sugar Act.

I must tell you then that I think the Parliament have overshot their mark & that you will not in the Event have your Expectations in any measure answered from the provisions of the late Act.

He believes "that the foreign Molasses will bear a Duty of One penny half penny at most."

I believe that the trade to the French & Dutch West Indies is failing & dying very fast & that there is not a single Voyage of that Sort planned with the most Distant intention to pay the Dutys. This brings me to remark upon one of your queries, viz. whether Smuggling can be Easily prevented here. I answer no. My reasons are [provided at length] but I verily believe there won't be Enough Collected in ye Course of ten years to Defray ye expence of fitting out one the least frigate for an American Voyage, & that the *whole Labour will be like burning a Barn to roast an Egg.*

Was the Duty lowered to where I have mentioned, the Merchants would pay it without any men of war to Compel him to it—he would pay it rather than run the risque of ye Custom house officer alone & partly by reason of his having been used to pay a Sum not much short of that [that is, because they have been paying that much in bribes and other costs of smuggling]. Perhaps 'tis the Intention of Parliament that *the Duty should amount to a prohibition of ye trade*—why they should Aim at that indeed I cannot conceive with the Ideas I now have of things.

To the degree the trade enriches the Americans it also enriches Great Britain.

What is the amount & Effect of that trade but the turning our horses, cattle, sheep, hogs, poultry, wheat, oats, Indian corn & Lumber of all sorts into Cash, & turning the same . . . into the hands of the British Merchant in payment for British manufactures.

He turns to the desire of the Americans to import British manufactures. It is hard to pay for luxuries without the means to do so—the trade restricted by the Sugar Act.

You will admit tis hard to be obliged to make brick without Straw. I wish I knew how & by what means we are to pay for the British manufactures which we are expected to purchase. We are as gay & Expensive as we possibly can be & only want the means to be more so.

He turns to the proposed stamp duties. He attacks the idea that the taxation is to support the British troops retained in America. The Americans can defend themselves; the expense of the British regiments is unnecessary. (This is a universal belief in America.)

What shall I Answer to your queries relative to the proposed internal taxation of America? You say America can & ought to Contribute to its own defence; we one & all say ye same on this Side ye water—we only differ about the means; we perhaps should first of all Rescind great part of the present Expence & what remains should difray by the Application of our own force & Strength.

It is hard to believe that the British will really take such an unwarranted step.

I will only remind you that our people dont yet believe that the British Parliament really mean to impose internal taxes upon us without our Consent, especially ye people of this Colony who . . . planted themselves & subsisted hitherto without one farthings Expence to ye Crown.

As an alternative to taxation, he suggests requisitions from the king.

If the King should fix the proportion of our Duty, we all say we will do our parts in ye Common Cause, but if the Parliament once interpose & Lay a tax, tho' it may be a very moderate one, & the Crown appoint officers of its own to Collect such tax & apply the same . . . what Consequences may, or rather may not, follow?

Next is a dramatic warning—that the Americans fear the precedent of the tax; even if the amount were reasonable at first, there was a danger of later uncontrollable and exorbitant increases.

The people think if the precedent is once established, Larger Sums may be Exacted & that at a time when the same shall be less needed, & *that in short you will have it in your power to keep us just as poor as you please.*

And he warns of the difficulty of collecting a tax that violates constitutional rights: "Contrary to the foundation principles of their natural & Constitutional rights & Liberties."

You see I am quite prevented from suggesting to you which of the Several methods of taxation that you mention would be the best or least Exceptionable, because I plainly perceive that every one of them or any supposable one, other than such as shall be laid by the Legislative bodies here . . . *would go down with the people like Chopt hay.*[7]

John Temple

On June 8, Whately wrote John Temple with a query about the planned stamp duty.

To us it appears ye most eligible of any, as being equal, extensive, not burthensome, likely to yield a considerable revenue, & collected without a great number of officers. Do you apprehend any material objections? & what do you guess it will raise, if imposed in any given proportion to ye same duty in England? You will pardon my inquisitiveness, but all these points are very interesting to me now, & you will oblige me by any information concerning them.[8]

Temple's response is of particular significance since he was an important British official in America. He was surveyor general of customs for the five northern colonies. The surveyor general was a revenue officer, a representative of the Commissioners of the Customs. He supervised the royal customs officers. (He is the same surveyor general alluded to at the end of chapter 1, on January 2, ordering strict compliance with the Molasses Act.) He was independent of the governor of any colony. He was often authorized by local courts to enter any ship or house to search for goods on which customs duties had not been paid. He was responsible for the prevention of piracy and illegal trade, and for providing an account to the king of goods forfeited.

In Temple's response of September 10, he took the occasion in the first part of the letter to discuss the Sugar Act, which was just a few weeks from coming into effect. Temple was optimistic about ending smuggling (one of his responsibilities) but pessimistic about revenue.

I think upon the whole that things are now in such a way that all kinds of smuggling & irregular trade will in a great measure soon be at an end. But I do not apprehend that the revenue that will be drawn from America will any way answer what seems to be the expectation of Ministry. I have paid all possible attention to the trade of this country, and have considered how the new act will probably operate. *Molosses is the principal article on which any money worth mentioning can be raised, & on that I fear Parliament will find they have left too large a duty in 3d a gallon.* The trade will either decline or methods will be found out thro corrupt officers in the West Indies to naturalize foreign produce there, & introduce it to the northern Colonies as Brittish growth.

So he, along with so many others, thinks the threepence duty is too high.

Next, he introduces a creative idea, including justification.

I could wish Parliament had left only 2d per gallon on molasses imported into the Colonies, & *that duty to have been general on the produce of Brittish as well as foreign molasses*; it certainly would have raised something handsome, & the duty, I believe, would have been punctually paid. Our own sugar planters could have no reasonable objection to the duty's being general, for *the molosses they export is so very inconsiderable that 'tis not worth mentioning.*

He explains that they export little molasses because they use it for their own production of rum.

With them 'tis all turned into rum, & principally sent to Great Brittain. Had the duty extended to molosses of what produce soever there would have been no possible means of its escaping the duty, & 2d a gallon, I believe, is full as much as the trade can bear & continue to flourish.

(His idea about the duty being lower, and also on British molasses, is prescient; Parliament acts on that idea in 1766.)

I come now to a more important affair, the stamp duty. This, I will suppose, as you say, is the most eligible & may be the most easily collected of any duty that can be laid, & will yield something handsome. On the same footing that it is in England, I suppose it will yield upwards of forty thousand pound sterling per annum in my district (the 5 Northern Colonies). But then for a moment consider Great Brittain & her Colonies on the larger scale, & see whither it will be either expedient or prudent to lay such a duty. It is a certain fact that the produce of all these Colonies in the course of trade goes now to Great Brittain for her manufactories, and if they produced three times as much as they do, it would all go for the same purpose.

This next observation is particularly significant in that he, a British official, agrees with the American claim that any revenue gained by taxation is lost to trade. He makes the specific point that the loss to trade is a pound-for-pound monetary loss.

Our people [Americans] are extravagantly fond of shew & dress, and have no bounds to their importation of Brittish manufactories but their want of money. Suppose a stamp tax to take place & to yield sixty thousand a year to be collected in America & sent home, *there would certainly be £60,000 worth of goods less imported from Great Brittain,* besides such a sum of money laying still in coffers for the Crown instead of circulating in the Colonies, already very much drained of cash.[9]

A STORM IS BREWING

While Grenville is dealing with the agents, and Halifax and Whately are receiving these return letters, patriot leaders in the colonies are formulating their response to Grenville's fifteenth resolution: essays and petitions that will fall heavy in London during the last months of 1764 and early 1765.

PART THREE

Protests

The colonies rejected all taxation by Parliament, any such an imposition being a violation of the rights of Englishmen, a violation of the constitutional right to be taxed only with their own consent or the consent of those who represent them. (We will see in every chapter an assertion of the need for such consent.) Americans saw Grenville's fifteenth resolution of March 9 as a threat to their liberty, as the first step toward economic slavery.

The renewal of the act of 1733, on the other hand, was generally seen as no change in policy; it had been renewed before. Just as in the original act, duties were given and granted to the king. A statement of purpose for "improving the revenue" was followed by "extending and securing the navigation and commerce." Even "necessary that a revenue be raised" did not ring alarm bells. The admonitions in 1763 from the secretary of state and the Board of Trade for improving the revenue seemed to be a repeat of previous exhortations to pay attention to the laws of trade. As a consequence, with few exceptions, Americans did not object to the duties of the Sugar Act as taxation. The Sugar Act of 1764, like its predecessor, was seen as trade regulation.[1]

Americans also dealt with a broader issue, one beyond the specific grievances: in 1763, "the balance of authority between metropolis and colonies remained undefined." As a consequence, the Americans began to reevaluate their constitutional relationship with Great Britain. The result? "The Stamp Act crisis of 1764–6 revealed a deep rift in understanding between the colonies and metropolis that would never be bridged within the structure of the empire."[2]

The next six chapters present the American protests on a colony-by-colony basis, but it is also useful to differentiate between the declarations of the colonies and the longer, more-thoughtful essays. There are nine declarations from the colonies and five essays.[3]

These essays, all distributed as pamphlets, began the reevaluation of the constitutional relationship with Great Britain.[4] James Otis: *The Rights of the British Colonies Asserted and Proved*; Oxenbridge Thacher: *The Sentiments of a British American*; Richard Bland: *The Colonel Dismounted . . . Containing a Dissertation upon the Constitution of the Colony*; Thomas Fitch: *Reasons why the British Colonies in America should not be charged with Internal Taxes*; Stephen Hopkins: *The Rights of Colonies Examined*.

Five

New York

N EW YORK WAS THE FIRST OF THE COLONIES TO PREPARE PETITIONS
to the king and Parliament. New York denied the authority
of Parliament to levy taxes on the colony and also denied the authority of Parliament to levy customs duties for the purpose of revenue.
The colony recognized the difference between the Molasses Act—to
which it had made no constitutional objection in April—and the
Sugar Act. Its objection was singular: New York was the only colony
to make a statement to Parliament that the duties of the Sugar Act
represented taxation.

ADDRESS OF THE ASSEMBLY

On September 4, 1764, Lieutenant Governor Colden opened the session of the assembly with a mundane recitation of minor governmental tasks. On September 11, the assembly responded. They start with
some mild comments and compliments to the king, "our most gracious Sovereign." Then an expression of confidence in his protecting
their rights transforms into this tirade against taxation. They hope
to be saved from,

> the deplorable state of that wretched people, who (being taxed by
> a power subordinate to none, and in a great degree unacquainted

with their circumstances) can call nothing their own. This we speak with the greatest deference to the wisdom and justice of the British Parliament.

After more general protest, they speak directly to the lieutenant governor.

We hope your Honor will join with us in an endeavour to secure that *great Badge of English Liberty of being taxed only with our Consent*; to which, we conceive, all His Majesty's Subjects at home and abroad equally entitled, and also in pointing out to the Ministry, the many mischiefs arising from the Act commonly called the Sugar Act, both to us and Great Britain.[1]

The forthright "taxed only with our Consent" denies the authority of Parliament. The British later called this address a declaration of "dangerous tendency" and an action that showed "indecent disrespect."

On September 17, Colden replied. "As the most material parts of this address cannot with any propriety be made to me, I shall transmit it to more proper judges of the sentiments you adopt."

The method you now take is, in my opinion, improper; however I shall do nothing to prevent your making a representation of the State of this Colony, which you think best. May your proceedings tend to the benefit of the people you represent.[2]

On September 19, the assembly appointed a committee to draw up a petition to the House of Commons "setting forth the many Inconveniences that must attend the infringing the Liberty we have so long enjoyed of being taxed only with our own Consent [and] that will arise from the Act commonly called the Sugar Act."[3]

A VIOLENT SPIRIT IN THE ASSEMBLY

On September 20, Colden wrote the Board of Trade, justifying why his response of September 17 was so mild and expressing his opinion regarding members of the assembly. It is important to interject some background here. There was a long-running political controversy in New York having to do with grants of large tracts of land. Colden suspects the controversy has fomented discontent among the representatives and prompted the forceful words of the assembly.

This Address of the Assembly appeared to me so *undutiful and indecent* that I think it incumbent on me to give your Lordships a particular account of my Conduct thereon. As soon as I discovered the tenor of the Address I endeavoured by every method in my power to *dissuade them from inserting suggestions which I think highly disrespectful to the Legislature of Great Britain*, for which there can be no foundation, & are inconsistent with that deference to the Wisdom & Justice of the British Parliament which they profess.

He did not want to decide alone on his next action. "I told the Assembly after they had presented their address to me, that I designed to have taken the Advice of the Council before I gave them an Answer."

It was unanimously agreed that the dissolving the Assembly could serve no good purpose, seeing I could not prevent the Publishing of the Address, for it was then actually Printed in a public Newspaper. A Dissolution would tend farther to inflame the Minds of the People [therefore] they advised me to give as soft an Answer as the Case would admit. Accordingly with their unanimous approbation I gave the answer of which the inclosed is a Copy.

This letter goes on at considerable length, discussing the nature of the men who have been elected as representatives.

It is my Duty to inform your Lordships from whence this violent Spirit arises so far as I can Judge from Circumstances and the Characters of the Men who at this time lead in the Assembly, & I shall now do it, tho' with the risque of the effects which the invenom'd Malice of Avarice & Ambition may produce.

Your Lordships have been inform'd of several extravagant Grants of Land in this Province.

The problem is, "The far greatest part of them still remain uncultivated, without any benefit to the Community, & are likewise a discouragement to the settling & improving the Lands in the neighbourhood of them."

Three of these great Tracts have in their Grants the Priviledge each in sending a Representative in general Assembly so that the Proprietors are become Hereditary Members of that House.

And the situation is similar for other representatives.

The General Assembly then of this Province consists of the Owners of these extravagant Grants, the Merchants of New York, the principal of them strongly connected with the Owners of these great Tracts by family Interest, & [the last group] of Common Farmers.

He asserts that the common farmers "are Men easily deluded & led away with popular Arguments of Liberty & Privilege."

The Proprietors of the great Tracts are not only freed from the Quit rent which the other Land holders in the Province Pay, but by their influence in the Assembly are *freed from every other public Tax on their Lands.*—While every Owner of improved Lands has every Horse, Cow, Ox, Hog, etc. and every Acre of his Land rated.

As a consequence, "Millions of Acres the Property of private Persons contribute nothing to the public necessary Expence."

The Proprietors of these large Tracts having been lately informed by their Correspondents in England that there is a design to Tax all the Lands equally for defraying the public charge, they have taken the alarm, & by every artifice inflame the Peoples Minds in hopes *thereby to deterr a British Parliament.*

That is, a policy of, "Tax all the Lands equally" would increase taxes for those with large tracts, but the owners of improved or cultivated lands (the *many* owners of such lands) would see reduced taxes. Therefore, he implies, the holders of large grants of land are motivated to raise the ire of the general population against a British land tax. But, he concludes, "I may assure your Lordships that the People of this Province before the present Sessions *were far from Entertaining the Sentiments contained in the Assembly's Address*."[4]

He paints a pretty negative picture of the representatives and their motives for opposing British initiatives. In fact, it is clear that he thought the constitutional rhetoric was "a mask for the fears of the great men who hoped to avoid paying taxes in the future as they had in the past."[5] Coloring his perception of their intent was that Colden was a particularly staunch imperialist, disinclined to see the virtue in legitimate constitutional arguments.

PETITIONS

The committee appointed to prepare a petition to the House of Commons took much bolder action than "setting forth the many Inconveniences" resulting from the taxation. On October 4, the assembly adopted the resulting petition without change and appointed committees to draft representations to the king and House of Lords. On October 18, the assembly approved all three petitions. The petition to the Commons is of most interest (and famous), but it is useful to start with small extracts from those to the king and the Lords.[6]

The King

The petition addresses three taxation issues: equality, right, and long usage. New York is a

> Dominion filled with Subjects, who esteem themselves happy in the firmest Attachment to your royal Person, Family and Government; the more happy, as under this Allegiance, they have had the highest Reason, from the hitherto uninterrupted Enjoyment of their civil Rights and Liberties as individuals, to consider themselves, in a State of *perfect Equality* with their fellow Subjects in Great Britain, and as a political Body, enjoying, like the Inhabitants of that Country, the *exclusive Right of Taxing themselves*; a Right, which with the most profound Submission be it spoken, whether inherent in the People, or sprung from any other Cause,

has received the royal Sanction, is at the Basis of our Colony State, and become *venerable by long Usage.*

Then the protest.

Your Majesty's faithful representatives for this your Colony of New-York, cannot, therefore, without the strongest Demonstrations of Grief, express their Sentiments on the late Intimation of a Design, to impose Taxes on your Majesty's Colonists, by Laws to be passed in Great-Britain.

In addition, the petition reprises the points made in the memorial of the previous April 20 (chapter 2) and makes a strong protest against admiralty courts and the limitation of the role of juries, the "antient badge of English Liberty."

The Lords

After a nearly hysterical recitation of problems, including the "utter destruction of our Liberties," the petitioners

represent to your Lordships that ever since the glorious Revolution, in which this Colony displayed the most distinguished Zeal and Alacrity, we have enjoyed the *uninterrupted Privilege, of being taxed only with our own consent, given by our Representatives in General Assembly.* This we have ever considered as the inextinguishable Right of British Subjects, because it is the natural Right of Mankind.

The Commons

This is the strongest statement of American rights approved by a legislative body and addressed to Parliament in 1764. Whatever the motivation of the representatives, the petition is famous, rightly so, as being a bold, uncompromising assertion of rights. It protested the duties of the Sugar Act as a violation of the rights of Americans.

To the Honourable the Knights, Citizens and Burgesses, representing the Commons of Great Britain, in Parliament assembled.

The Representation and Petition of the General-Assembly of the Colony of New York.

The petition starts with a preamble, a basis for rights the New Yorkers are going to claim.

Most humbly Shew,
   That from the Year 1683, to this Day, there have been three Legislative Branches in this Colony; consisting of the Governor and Council appointed by the Crown, and the Representatives chosen by the People, who, besides the Power of making Laws for the Colony, *have enjoyed the Right of Taxing the Subject for the Support of the Government.*

Considering the importance of precedent, this long period of (exclusive) right of taxation essentially makes it part of the New York constitution.

Under this Political Frame, the Colony was settled by Protestant Emigrants from several Parts of Europe, and more especially from Great Britain and Ireland: And as it was originally modeled with the Intervention of the Crown, and not excepted to by the Realm of England before, nor by Great Britain since the Union, the Planters and Settlers conceived the strongest Hopes that the Colony had gained a *civil Constitution*, which, so far at least as the Rights and Privileges of the People were concerned, *would remain permanent*, and be transmitted to their latest Posterity.

Here is the main point: continued freedom from British taxation. First, the economic argument against taxation.

It is therefore with equal Concern and Surprize, that they have received Intimations of certain Designs lately formed, if possible, to induce the Parliament of Great Britain, to *impose Taxes upon the Subjects here, by Laws to be passed there*; and as we who have the Honour to represent them conceive that this Innovation will greatly affect the Interest of the Crown and the Nation, and reduce the Colony to absolute Ruin; it became our indispensable Duty to trouble you with a reasonable Representation of the Claim of our Constituents *to an Exemption from the Burthen of all Taxes not granted by themselves.*

(The claim of exemption from all taxes goes beyond the committee's mandate to simply point out the inconveniences of taxation by Parliament.)

Had the Freedom from all Taxes not granted by ourselves been enjoyed as a Privilege, we are confident the Wisdom and Justice of the British Parliament would rather establish than destroy it, unless by our abuse of it the Forfeiture was justly incurred; but his Majesty's Colony of New York can not only defy the whole World to impeach their Fidelity, but appeal to all the Records of their past Transactions as well for the fullest Proof of their steady Affection to the Mother Country.

Here is the second argument against taxation, a matter of principle. They argue from the point of view of natural right.

But an Exemption from the Burthen of ungranted, involuntary Taxes must be the grand Principle of every free State. *Without such a Right vested in themselves, exclusive of all others, there can be no Liberty, no Happiness, no Security;* it is inseparable from the very Idea of Property, for who can call that his own which may be taken away at the Pleasure of another? And so evidently does this appear to be *the natural Right of Mankind*, that even conquered tributary States, though subject to the Payment of a fixed periodical Tribute, never were reduced so abject and forlorn a Condition as to yield to all the Burthens which their Conquerors might at any future Time think fit to impose.

May we proceed to inform the Commons of Great Britain . . . that the People of this Colony, inspired by the Genius of their Mother Country, nobly *disdain the thought of claiming that Exemption as a Privilege.* They found it on a Basis more honourable, solid and stable; they challenge it, and *glory in it as their Right.*

The right is the same as subjects in Great Britain; the Americans ought not to be treated differently, particularly since they have suffered "unutterable Hardships" on behalf of the empire.

That [freedom from involuntary taxation] may be exercised by his Majesty's Subjects at Home, and justly denied to those who submitted to Poverty, Barbarian Wars, Loss of Blood, Loss of Money, personal Fatigues, and ten Thousand unutterable Hardships . . . no Sophistry can recommend to the Sober, impartial Decision of common Sense.

They next allude to the fact that Britain has a balanced legislature: king—Lords—Commons.

Our Constituents exult in that glorious Model of Government [with] Distribution of the Power of the Nation in the three great Legislative Branches.

They go on to make the point that there is an advantage to being taxed by the power of the Crown: a king will not favor one part of the kingdom over another. But this is not the current situation at all. Since a Parliament *there* is taxing a people *here*, the burden will be unjust, even tyrannical. "No History can furnish an Instance of a Constitution to permit one Part of a Dominion to be taxed by another, and that too in Effect, but by a Branch of that other Part."

The petition advocates for retention of the traditional process of raising a revenue from the colonies—requisition from the Crown—and makes the all-but-required statement that New York has no "desire of Independency." Next is a transition to issues of trade and duties.

What can be more apparent, than that the State which exercises a Sovereignty in Commerce, can draw all the Wealth of its Colonies into its own Stock? And has not the whole Trade of North-America, that growing Magazine of Wealth, been, from the Beginning, directed, restrained, and prohibited at the sole Pleasure of the Parliament? And whatever some may pretend, his Majesty's American

Subjects are far from a Desire to invade the just Rights of Great Britain, in all commercial Regulations. They humbly conceive, that a very *manifest Distinction presents itself*, which, while it leaves to the Mother Country an incontestable Power, to give Laws for the Advancement of her own Commerce, will, at the same Time, do no Violence to the Rights of the Plantations.

Here is an explicit yielding of authority for trade regulation.

The Authority of the Parliament of Great Britain to *model the Trade of the whole Empire* so as to subserve the Interest of her own, we are ready to recognize in the most extensive and positive Terms. [For example, the colonies] would not ask for a Licence to import woolen Manufactures from France; or to go into the most lucrative Branches of Commerce in the least Degree incompatible with the Trade and Interest of Great Britain.

But such authority is limited.

But a Freedom to drive all Kinds of Traffick in a Subordination to, and not inconsistent with, the British Trade; and an Exemption from all Duties in such a Course of Commerce, is humbly claimed by the Colonies as *the most essential of all the Rights to which they are intitled*, as Colonists from, and connected, in the common Bond of Liberty with the *unenslaved Sons of Great Britain*.

Let me make that more specific to our story: a duty on "Traffick" (such as molasses) that does not interfere (is not inconsistent) with British trade violates "the most essential of all the Rights to which they are intitled." This is a rare objection that such duties violate American rights. The assertion is not explicit, does not use the word *tax* here, but there can be no question of the meaning. Continuing this theme, here is the absolute objection to *any* tax, including duties (for revenue).

Since all Impositions, *whether they be internal Taxes or Duties paid* for what we consume, equally diminish the Estates upon which they are charged; what avails it to any People, by which of them they are impoverished? Every Thing will be given up to preserve Life; and though there is a Diversity in the Means, *yet, the whole Wealth of a Country may be as effectually drawn off by the Exaction of Duties, as by any other Tax upon their Estates.*

New York does not condone attempts to draw off the wealth of the country "by the Exaction of Duties" but instead decries such actions as unjust: such power must remain in the hands of the colony.

And therefore, the General Assembly of New York, in Fidelity to their Constituents, cannot but express the most earnest Supplication, that the Parliament will charge our Commerce with *no other Duties than a necessary Regard* to the particular Trade of Great Britain evidently demands; but leave it to the legislative Power of the Colony to impose all other Burthens upon it's own People, which the publick Exigences may require.

They do not use the phrase *duties for revenue*, but certainly such a duty as the molasses duty (being intended to raise revenue for "publick Exigences") falls outside "a necessary Regard to the particular Trade of Great Britain" and is therefore equivalent to a tax. This section highlights that the Sugar Act infringed colonial rights "by imposing duties on branches of colonial commerce which did not conflict with British interests." Although Parliament has power to regulate trade, this action was an abuse of that power.

The insistence that other impositions be left "to the legislative Power of the Colony" limits the reach of Parliament, reinforces that duties for revenue constitute taxation, and emphasizes the exclusive taxing power of the colony to support its internal government. Here is a bit of wry understatement.

Latterly, the Laws of Trade seem to have been framed without an Attention to this fundamental Claim.

The petition goes on to make grandiose statements about the contributions of America to the wealth of Great Britain. "All our Riches

must flow into Great Britain. Immense have been our Contributions
to the National Stock." This following colorful turn of phrase emphasizes submission to regulations that enrich the mother country.

> We carry all to her Hive, and consume the Returns; and we are
> content with any *constitutional* Regulation that inriches her,
> though it impoverishes ourselves.

Presumably, constitutional regulations are those that impose "no
other Duties than a necessary Regard to the particular Trade of Great
Britain evidently demands."

There are economic problems with the Sugar Act.

> The Act of the last Session of Parliament, inhibiting all Intercourse
> between the Continent and the foreign Sugar Colonies, will prove
> equally detrimental to us and Great Britain. That Trade gave a
> value to a vast, but now alas unsaleable Staple [i.e., New York
> products], which being there converted into Cash and Merchan-
> dize, made necessary Remittances for the British Manufactures we
> consumed.

The petition goes on, but I will skip to this most dramatic climax.

> The General Assembly of this Colony have no desire to derogate
> from the Power of the Parliament of Great Britain; but they cannot
> avoid deprecating the Loss of such Rights as they have hitherto
> enjoyed, Rights established in the first Dawn of our Constitution,
> founded upon the most substantial Reasons, confirmed by invari-
> able Usage, conducive to the best Ends; never abused to bad Pur-
> poses, and with the Loss of which Liberty, Property, and all the
> Benefits of Life, tumble into Insecurity and Ruin: Rights, the Dep-
> rivation of which, *will dispirit the People, abate their Industry,
> discourage Trade, introduce Discord, Poverty and Slavery*; or, by
> depopulating the Colonies, turn a vast, fertile, prosperous Region,
> into a dreary Wilderness, impoverish Great Britain, and *shake the
> Power and Independency of the most opulent and flourishing Em-
> pire in the World.*

The statement nicely illustrates the tension seen in many American petitions. Flattery: They "have no desire to derogate from the Power." Protest: "the Loss of such Rights," will ultimately "dispirit the People." Threat: "shake the Power" of the empire. The petition winds down with a flourish of further flattery and submission, simply showing respect for the institution of Parliament.

All which your Petitioners (who repose the highest Confidence in your Wisdom and Justice) humbly pray.

Here we expect to see a demand to repeal the Sugar Act and not impose stamp duties, but the ending is more subtle, requesting the House of Commons to take all the above into consideration and pursue such measures "as the Event may prove to have been concerted for the Common-Weal of all the Subjects of Great Britain, both at home and abroad." The petition is formalized with, "By Order of the General Assembly, Wm. Nicoll, Speaker. City of New-York, Oct. 18, 1764."

Taken as a whole, the petition is a clear denial of the authority of Parliament to tax New York, either by internal taxes or inappropriate duties ("as by any other Tax"). It admits the authority of Parliament to regulate trade (even to the advantage of Britain), including the imposition of duties. But Parliament must not go beyond such regulation; if a duty is enacted for the purpose of revenue, it is a violation of colonial rights, making the Sugar Act an unconstitutional money bill.

The petitions were sent to New York agent Robert Charles on October 18.

RESULT OF THE PETITIONS

The petitions had no effect. The one to the Commons was never presented to the House, one agent putting it this way about the efforts of Charles to enlist a sponsor: the petition "was conceived in terms so inflammatory that he could not prevail on any one Member of the House to present it."[7]

Six

Massachusetts

THE POPULAR LEADERS (OR PATRIOTS, OR RADICALS, OR—eventually—revolutionaries) of Massachusetts were the earliest and most vocal of the protestors. They were in control of the House of Representatives and were quick to state grievances, including a draft address to the king and Parliament. Two of their prominent members, James Otis and Oxenbridge Thacher, created pamphlets in protest of the British actions. The colony also prepared a petition (to the House of Commons only) and sent conflicting instructions to the colony's agent.

BOSTON TOWN MEETING, MAY 24

By mid-May, the Grenville resolutions of March 9 and 10 had arrived in Boston. At a Boston Town Meeting of May 24, a committee led by Samuel Adams prepared instructions to the Boston delegates in the Massachusetts legislature (including Otis, Thacher, and Thomas Cushing). The instructions are critical of the delay in dealing with "the intention of the ministry to burden us with new taxes." They stress, "There is now no room for further delay; we therefore expect that you will use your earliest endeavours in the General Assembly that such methods may be taken as will effectually prevent these proceedings against us." And the committee hopes "for a repeal of the act, should it be already pass'd."

Here is a stirring expression of dread that exemplifies American concerns during 1764.

> What still heightens our apprehensions is that these unexpected proceedings may be preparatory to new taxations upon us; for if our trade may be taxed, why not our lands? Why not the produce of our lands and everything we possess or make use of? This we apprehend annihilates our charter right to govern and tax ourselves. It strikes at our British privileges, which, as we have never forfeited them, we hold in common with our fellow subjects who are natives of Britain. If *taxes are laid upon us in any shape without our having a legal representation where they are laid*, are we not reduced from the character of free subjects to the miserable state of tributary slaves?

And at the end:

> As his Majesty's other northern American colonies are embark'd with us in this most important bottom, we further desire you to use your endeavors, that their weight may be added to that of this province: that by the united application of all who are aggrieved, All may happily obtain redress.[1]

SUMMER IN MASSACHUSETTS

Summer 1764 brought forth a torrent of paper that anticipates much of the discussion in following years.

Letter to Agent Mauduit

The House of Representatives (the Assembly) convened on May 30, 1764.

> Mr. Speaker communicated sundry Letters from Mr. Agent Mauduit Dated London, [September through March] together with sundry Papers inclosed, which were read.
>
> Ordered, That [a committee, including Otis, Thacher, Cushing]

take the Letters and Papers under Consideration, together with
the Letters receiv'd last Year, and make Report.[2]

On June 13, the committee submitted its work, "which was read
and accepted, and is as follows."

The House of Representatives have received your several Letters
of the 30th of December, the 11th of February, the 13th of March
and the 23d of March last. *The Contents are to the last degree
alarming.* In that of the 30th of December, you seem to wonder at
the silence of the House.

(This is the letter we saw in chapter 1 in which Jasper said, "The
General Court have not been pleased to instruct me in their sentiments upon this subject.")

Volumes have been transmitted from this Province in relation to
the Sugar Act, to little Purpose. If a West-Indian, or any other bye
Influence is to govern and supersede our most essential Rights as
British Subjects, what will it avail us to make Remonstrances, or
the most demonstrable Representations of our Rights and Priviledges. You "hope however there will be found a general disposition to serve the Colonies, and not to distress them." The sudden
passing of the Sugar-Act, and continuing a heavy Duty on that
Branch of our Commerce, we are far from thinking a Proof that
your Hope had any solid Foundation.

Mauduit took unapproved and inappropriate action.

No Agent of this Province has Power to make express concessions
in any case without express Orders. And the Silence of the
Province should have been imputed to any Cause, even to Dispair,
rather than be construed into a tacit Cession of their Rights, or
an Acknowledgment of a Right in the Parliament of Great-Britain
to *impose Duties and Taxes upon a People who are not represented in the House of Commons.*

The criticism grows ever more harsh.

The Letter of the 11th of February is still more surprising. We conceive nothing could restrain your liberty of opposing so burthensome a scheme, as that of obliging the Colonies to maintain an army. *What merit could there be in a submission to such an unconstitutional measure?* . . . Is there any thing in your power of agency, or in the nature of the office, that can warrant a concession of this kind? Most certainly there is not.

They lecture him regarding rights.

If all the colonists are to be taxed at pleasure without any representatives in parliament, what will there be to distinguish them, in point of liberty, from the subjects of the most absolute prince? *If we are to be taxed at pleasure, without our consent, will it be any consolation to us, that we are to be assessed by a hundred instead of one? If we are not represented, we are slaves.*

They address the delay in imposition of the stamp duties.

The actual laying the stamp duty, you say, is deferred 'till next year, Mr. Grenville being willing to give the Provinces their option to raise that or some other equivalent tax, "desirous," as he was pleased to express himself, "to consult the Ease, the Quiet and Good-will of the Colonies."
  If the Ease, the Quiet and Good-will of the Colonies are of any Importance to Great Britain, no measures could be hit upon that have a more natural and direct tendency to enervate those principles, than the resolutions you inclose.

This next comment demonstrates that these leaders understood the fifteenth resolution to be an all but formal plan.

The kind offer of suspending this stamp duty in the manner and upon the condition you mention, amounts to no more than this; *that if the Colonies will not tax themselves as they may be directed, the parliament will tax them.*

Despite the earlier objection regarding his flawed "acknowledgment of a Right in the Parliament of Great Britain to impose Duties and Taxes," the house offers this quibble, not about rights but about the amount of the duty and its purpose.

> We find by yours of the 23d that the Necessities of the Publick would not admit of the Duty on Molasses being set lower than Three Pence. This seems to us to be a little repugnant to the Assurances given in your former Letter from the Ministry, that the Colonies were not to be Taxed for the Support of the Government at Home.

They take a side trip to discuss the proper amount of duty.

> The Duty in all good Policy should have been low at first, if it was right to lay any. It might have been increased by Degrees as it would bear. But in this way is probable, that not a tenth Part of the Money will be collected as at a Penny. The Business, if it will bear any Thing, will admit but of a light Duty.

A high duty will result in molasses being brought in by smuggling.

> People on a Continent of three Thousand Miles, filled with Bays, Ports and Creeks, will find Means to elude the Vigilance of the most Eagle-eyed Officers, unless Guard ships and Custom-House Officers are increased to such a Number as to eat up the whole Duty.

The letter eventually includes direct instructions.

> You are to remonstrate against these measures, and if possible, to obtain a repeal of the Sugar Act, and prevent the imposition of any further Duties or Taxes on these Colonies. Measures will be taken that you may be joined by all the other agents.

The "measures will be taken" is a letter to other colonies (sent on June 25). The instructions are briefly interrupted to give Mauduit a little balm for the wounds inflicted.

The House must do you the Justice to admit that you gave sufficient hints of the intended measures to alarm us: But it was not
conceived that these measures would be so suddenly carried into
execution.

Then more lecturing.

It may be said that if the Parliament have a Right to lay Prohibitions they can certainly lay Duties, which is a less Burthen. [But]
let it be remembered that equity and justice require that the power
of laying prohibitions on the dominions who are not represented
in Parliament should be exercised with great moderation. But this
had better be exercised with the utmost rigour than the *power of
taxing: for this last is the grand barrier of British liberty*; which if
once broken down, all is lost.

In a word, a people may be free and tolerably happy without a
particular branch of trade, but without the privilege of assessing
their own taxes, they can be neither.

Ending with more direction.

Inclosed you will have a brief *State of the Rights of the British
Colonies*, drawn up by one of our members, which you are to
make the best use of in your power, with the addition of such arguments as your own good sense will suggest.[3]

The document enclosed had been prepared by James Otis. I will
discuss it shortly, in a separate section.

The letter to Mauduit of June 13 was momentous, marking the
start of increased independent action by the assembly. Lieutenant
Governor Thomas Hutchinson later wrote that this independent action (choosing to not coordinate with the council or governor)
"seems to have *been the first instance* of any act of the House of Representatives, separate from the other branches, in any matter of importance" to the colony as a whole.[4]

CALL FOR UNITED ACTION

On June 25, the assembly wrote the other colonies. They deal with "the late Act of Parliament relating to the Sugar Trade with Foreign Colonies, and the Resolutions of the House of Commons relating to Stamp Duties and other Taxes proposed to be laid on the British colonies." (This is a famous and influential letter; I will refer to it in following chapters.)

Those measures have a tendency to deprive the colonists of *some of their most essential rights as British subjects and as men*, particularly the right of assessing their own taxes, and being free from any impositions but such as they consent to by themselves, or representatives.

Our Agent informs us, that in a Conference he had with Mr. Grenville on these Subjects, he was told that the Ministry were desirous of consulting the Ease, the Quiet and Goodwill of the Colonies.

Such Expressions induce us to hope that there is Nothing punitive in these Measures, and that humble dutiful Remonstrances may yet have their Effect. But if while these Things are thus publickly handled, no Claim is made, no Remonstrance preferred on the Part of the Colonies, such Silence must be interpreted a tacit Cession of their Rights, and an humble Acquiescence under all these Burdens.

The House have wrote fully upon this Subject to the Agent of this Province, and directed him to remonstrate against these Measures, and to endeavour a Repeal of said Act, and if possible to prevent the Imposition of any further Duties and Taxes on the Colonies.

They advocate united action.

For this Purpose they were desirous of the united Assistance of the several Colonies in a Petition against such formidable Attacks upon what they conceive to be the inseparable Rights of British Subjects; and that the Agents of the several Colonies might be directed by the Representatives of the People on the Continent of

North America to unite in the most serious Remonstrance against Measures so destructive of the Liberty, the Commerce and Property of the Colonists, and in their Tendency so pernicious to the real Interest of Great Britain.[5]

On June 29, Governor Bernard sent to the Board of Trade copies of the June 13 and June 25 letters. He added these comments on the letter to other governments.

Altho' this may seem at first sight only an occasional measure for a particular purpose, yet I have reason to believe that the purposes it is to serve are deeper than they now appear. I apprehend that it is intended to take this opportunity to make a schism in the General Court to be enlarged [and] to lay a foundation for connecting the demagogues of the several Governments in America to *join together in opposition to all orders from Great Britain which don't square with their notions of the rights of the people.* Perhaps I may be too suspicious; a little time will show whether I am or not.[6]

Bernard understood this to be a pivotal moment; he sees the beginning of the Americans assuming a right to judge the appropriateness of orders from Great Britain, and to jointly oppose those orders. Time showed he was not too suspicious.

The Memorial by James Otis

The *State of the Rights of the British Colonies* by James Otis enclosed in the June 13 letter to Mauduit is a valuable essay in its own right and a springboard to a longer document I present below. (It is also an appendix to the longer document.)

James Otis was an important character, a political and intellectual leader. John Adams, writing to a friend in 1818, said this about him.

Mr. Otis roundly asserted this whole system of parliamentary regulations . . . to be illegal, unconstitutional, tyrannical, null, and void.

Nevertheless, with all my admiration of Mr. Otis, and enthusiasm for his character, I must acknowledge he was not always consistent in drawing or admitting the *necessary consequences* from his principles, one of which comprehended them all, to wit, that *Parliament had no authority over America in any case whatsoever.*[7]

Otis's argument is based on natural rights: laws of nature and God, as established in the British constitution ("in affirmance of the common law and law of nature"). The rights go back to 1215. "The absolute *rights of Englishmen,* as frequently declared in Parliament, from Magna Charta, to this time, are the rights of personal security, personal liberty and of private property."[8]

> By the laws of nature and of nations, by the voice of universal reason, and of God, when a nation takes possession of a desart, uncultivated, uninhabited country [the colonists are] entitled to all the essential rights of the mother country.
>
> The colonists have been by their several charters declared natural subjects, and entrusted with the power of making their own local laws, not repugnant to the laws of England, and with the power of taxing themselves.

Otis argues "that the power of the British Parliament is held as sacred and as uncontrollable in the colonies as in England," but yet there are limits on that power.

> The question is not upon the general power or right of the Parliament, but whether it is not circumscribed within some equitable and reasonable bounds. 'Tis hoped it will not be considered as a new doctrine that even the authority of the Parliament of Great Britain is circumscribed by certain bounds which *if exceeded their acts become those of mere power without right, and consequently void.* The judges of England have declared in favor of these sentiments when they expressly declare that acts of Parliament against natural equity are void. *That acts against the fundamental principles of the British constitution are void.*

Eventually, the memorial reprises the arguments made early in the year (in the *Reasons against the renewal* pamphlet) to rant against the economic burden of the new Sugar Act, giving Mauduit ammunition to lobby for its repeal. Otis adds new information, relying on an authoritative British writer to claim "that one half of the immense commerce of Great Britain is with her colonies. It is very certain that without the fishery seven eighths of this commerce would cease."

> Without the French West-India produce . . . our fishery must infallibly be ruined. . . . A few years experience of the execution of the Sugar Act will sufficiently convince the Parliament not only of the inutility but destructive tendency of it. . . . That the trade with the colonies has been of surprising advantage to Great Britain notwithstanding the want of a good regulation is past all doubt. Great Britain is well known to have increased prodigiously both in numbers and in wealth since she began to colonize."

He continues at great length, advancing this objection to duties. "I believe every duty that was ever imposed on commerce, or in the nature of things can be, will be found to be divided between the state imposing the duty and the country exported from." It is therefore senseless to impose duties on products traded within the British Empire. Eventually, at the end, he is emphatic that the West Indies trade is beneficial.

> The only test of a useful commodity is the gain upon the whole to the state; such should be free. The only test of a pernicious trade is the loss upon the whole or to the community; this [trade] should be prohibited [only if] it can be demonstrated that the sugar and molasses trade from the northern colonies to the foreign plantations is upon the whole a loss to the community. . . . This never has been proved, nor can be, the contrary being certain.

The Pamphlet by James Otis

One of the most widely read and discussed pamphlets of this period was Otis's *The Rights of the British Colonies Asserted and Proved*, published in Boston, July 23, 1764. Written at the same time as essays by Oxenbridge Thacher, Stephen Hopkins, and Thomas Fitch, "it surpassed them all in fame, and also in ambiguity of meaning and

in the variety of interpretations given to it."[9] Hutchinson, in a letter
to Richard Jackson, called it "a loose, unconnected performance."
And a prominent Connecticut lawyer said it "conceded away the
rights of America."

Otis establishes that Parliament has supreme power. ("The power
of Parliament is uncontrollable but by themselves.") However, most
important for our story, is that although it can do anything, it cannot
tax America. His resolution of the apparent contradiction is that ultimately, Parliament will make no unjust law—no law against right
and equity. If, through misinformation such law is nonetheless enacted, Parliament will correct the error when convinced of the correct
path.

Otis starts with a long exposition on the origin and form of government, eventually getting to this idea.

> I affirm that government is founded on the necessity of our natures
> and that an *original supreme, sovereign, absolute, and uncontrol-*
> *lable earthly power must exist in and preside over every society,*
> from whose final decisions there can be no appeal but directly to
> Heaven. It is therefore originally and ultimately in the people.

He has more to say on government.

> The end of government being the good of mankind, points out its
> great duties. It is above all things to provide for the security, the
> quiet, and happy enjoyment of life, liberty, and property. . . . The
> first principle and great end of government being to provide for
> the best good of all the people, this can be done only by a supreme
> legislative and executive ultimately in the people.

It being impractical to gather large groups of people, the power is
necessarily executed through representatives—which introduces a de-
rivative right: "a right of representation." Otis ends that line of
thought with two quotations from John Locke. "There can be but
one supreme power which is the legislative, to which all the rest are
and must be subordinate." Nonetheless, "The natural liberty of man
is to be free from any superior power on earth, and not to be under

the will or legislative authority of man, but only to have the law of nature for his rule."

We have reached the central point of the essay, a section that Otis calls "The Political and Civil Rights of the British Colonists." He starts, "The Parliament of Great Britain has an undoubted *power and lawful authority* to make acts for the general good." Such acts of Parliament are "equally binding [on Americans] as upon the subjects of Great Britain within the realm."

The colonists are entitled "to all the natural, essential, and inseparable rights of our fellow subjects in Great Britain." These cannot be taken away. Next, he states a number of rights, and then sets this limit (among others) on the rightful authority of Parliament.

The supreme power cannot take from any man any part of his property without his consent in person or by representation.

He restates that the rights place a limit on Parliament. "These are their bounds, which by God and nature are fixed; hitherto have they a right to come, and no further." He is specific about taxes. "Taxes are not to be laid on the people but by their consent in person or by deputation." (This takes only a bit of reshaping to come out as: *no taxation without representation.*)

These are the first principles of law and justice, and the great barriers of a free state and of the British constitution in particular. I ask, I want, no more.

He reemphasizes the liberties of colonists, of all colonists.

That the colonists, black and white, born here, are free born British subjects, and entitled to all the essential civil rights of such, is a truth not only manifest from the provincial charters, from the principles of the common law, and acts of parliament; but from the British constitution.[10]

And further, "no one ever dreamt, surely, that these liberties were confined to the realm."

Property is the foundation of liberty. "Now can there be any liberty, where property is taken away without consent?" In consequence, although Parliament is supreme, although Parliament can impose restrictions and even prohibition on colonial trade, it cannot levy taxes (including port duties) on the unrepresented colonies.

I can see no reason to doubt but that the imposition of taxes, whether on trade, or on land, or houses, or ships, on real or personal, fixed or floating property, in the colonies is absolutely irreconcilable with the rights of the colonists as British subjects and as men.

Freedom from taxation is an essential right. "The very act of taxing exercised over those who are not represented appears to me to be depriving them of one of their most essential rights as freemen." He later returns to a train of thought in which he emphasizes the power of Parliament.

With regard to the Parliament, as infallibility belongs not to mortals, 'tis possible they may have been misinformed and deceived. *The power of Parliament is uncontrollable but by themselves, and we must obey. They only can repeal their own acts.*

Although Parliament may be misinformed or deceived in the short term, they "always will"—as a result of their wisdom and justice—correct the error and repeal any unjust act. But until they do, "it is our duty to submit and patiently bear them, till they will be pleased to relieve us."

And tis to be presumed, the wisdom and justice of that august assembly, always will afford us relief by repealing such acts, as through mistake or other human infirmities, have been suffered to pass, *if they can be convinced* that their proceedings are not constitutional, or not for the common good.

He laments the recent lack of protest against the Sugar Act. It seems as though there is acceptance of the recent duties since they are a tax on trade. "There has been a most profound and I think shameful silence, till it seems almost too late to assert our indisputable rights as men and as citizens." Continued silence can lead to greater woes. "I cannot but observe here, that *if the parliament have an equitable right to tax our trade*, 'tis indisputable that they have as good an one to tax the lands, and *everything else*."

Otis claims that the situation is confusing because of a fundamental misunderstanding. "There is no foundation for the distinction some make in England between an internal and an external tax on the colonies." Otis disallows duties as being unjust, being the same as taxes. If it can lay duties on trade, "why may not the parliament lay stamps, land taxes [and so on]. I know of no bounds."

He eventually returns to the idea that although Parliament is supreme, there are some things it cannot do.

> To say the parliament is absolute and arbitrary is a contradiction. *The parliament cannot make 2 and 2, 5; Omnipotence cannot do it.* . . . Parliaments are in all cases to declare what is for the good of the whole; but it is not the declaration of Parliament that makes it so [but God, or natural law]. Should an act of parliament be against any . . . natural laws, which are immutably true, their declaration would be contrary to eternal truth, equity and justice, and consequently void: and so it would be adjudged by the parliament itself, when convinced of their mistake.
>
> Upon this great principle, parliaments repeal such acts, as soon as they find they have been mistaken, in having declared them to be for the public good, when in fact they were not so.

He is convinced this will all work out. Indeed, everything is wonderful!

> See here the grandeur of the British constitution! See the wisdom of our ancestors! The supreme legislative and the supreme executive are a perpetual check and balance to each other. If the supreme executive errs it is informed by the supreme legislative in Parliament. If the supreme legislative errs it is informed by the supreme executive in the King's courts of law. . . . This is government! This is a constitution!

He makes clear his opinion about prohibitions on trade (OK), as opposed to taxation (not OK). "Admitting the right of prohibition, in its utmost extent and latitude; a *right of taxation can never be inferred* from that."

> Though it be allowed, that liberty may be enjoyed in a comfortable measure where prohibitions are laid on the trade of a kingdom or province, yet if taxes are laid on either without consent, they cannot be said to be free. This barrier of liberty being once broken down, all is lost. If a shilling in the pound may be taken from me against my will, why may not twenty shillings; and if so, why not my liberty or my life?

This assertion is directly opposite to the belief of Richard Jackson. In chapter 1, we saw his statement (December 27, 1763): since "the mother country may prohibit foreign Trade, it may therefore tax it."

Otis allows as how trade is free in England, that merchants were favored by the common law. He then asks, "And why not as well to the plantations? Are they not entitled to all the British privileges?" His answer yields much to the supremacy of Parliament.

> No, they must be confined in their imports and exports to the good of the metropolis. Very well, we have submitted to this. The act of navigation is a good act, so are all that exclude foreign manufactures from the plantations, and every honest man will readily subscribe to them.

He eventually turns to the Molasses Act (1733). He has mixed feelings about duties for the regulation of trade, but, consistent with the assertions above, no hesitation about prohibition.

> The act of the 6th of his late Majesty, tho' it imposes a *duty* in terms, has been said to be designed for a *prohibition*, which is probable from the sums imposed; and 'tis pity it had not been so expressed, as there is not the least doubt of the just and equitable right of the parliament to lay prohibitions through the dominions when they think the good of the whole requires it.

He has no new comment about the recent Sugar Act.

It is said that the duties imposed by the new act will amount to a prohibition: time only can ascertain this. The utility of this act is so fully examined in the Appendix, that I shall add nothing on that head here.

(We saw his opinion of the "utility" of the act, referring to the "destructive tendency of it.")

In order to emphasize that the colonies are under the authority of Parliament, he discusses the empire-shaking events of seventeenth-century England, concluding that Parliament is "the supreme legislative of Great Britain . . . and the dominions thereto belonging." But although supreme, the British constitution decrees that Parliament cannot levy taxes without consent of those taxed.

[And] that this constitution is the most free one, and by far the best, now existing on earth; That by this constitution every man in the dominions is a free man; *That no parts of His Majesty's dominions can be taxed without their consent*; That every part has a right to be represented in the supreme or some subordinate legislature.

After that buildup about representation, he suggests that the Americans be represented in Parliament (a distinctly minority opinion in America). He ends on that note, that it would result in "the greatest peace and prosperity."

The essay is followed by his earlier *State of the Rights of the British Colonies* as an appendix, with this preface.

Substance of a Memorial presented the Assembly . . . and by the House voted to be transmitted to Jasper Mauduit, Esq., Agent for This Province; to be improved as he may judge proper.[11]

Oxenbridge Thacher: The Sentiments of a British American

The Sentiments of a British American was written in summer 1764 by Oxenbridge Thacher. (The essay was published as a pamphlet on September 3.) Thacher protested not only the economic effect of the

Sugar Act but also its nature as unconstitutional taxation. He was one of those few (well, not so few in Massachusetts) who early on "recognized the constitutional connection. It was not a matter of trade or costs; it was a matter of the constitutional right to be taxed only by consent."[12] Thacher was the first major essayist to be explicit that the Sugar Act levied a tax, denoting (along with the extensive regulation of trade) a radical change in the relationship between Great Britain and its American colonies.

He starts by establishing the importance of colonies—of America—and the contribution to the "heighth of glory and wealth" of the empire. The colonies have "contributed to the advancing and increasing its grandeur from their very first beginnings."

> In the forming and settling, therefore, the internal polity of the kingdom, these have reason to expect that their interest should be considered and attended to, that their rights, if they have any, should be preserved to them.

They hold the inherent rights of Englishmen, "having the same British rights."

> The writer of this, being a native of an English colony, will take it for granted that the colonies are not the mere property of the mother state; that they have the same rights as other British subjects. He will also suppose that no design is formed to enslave them, and that the justice of the British Parliament will finally do right to every part of their dominions.
>
> These things presupposed, he intends to consider the [Sugar Act] to show the real subjects of grievance therein to the colonists, and that the interest of Great Britain itself may finally be greatly affected thereby. There is the more reason that this freedom should be indulged after the act is passed inasmuch as the colonies, though greatly interested therein, had no opportunity of being heard while it was pending.

Here is his principal argument, unblushingly calling out the duties of the Sugar Act as taxes.

The first objection is that a tax is thereby laid on several commodities, to be raised and levied in the plantations, and to be remitted home to England. This is esteemed a grievance inasmuch as the same are laid without the consent of the representatives of the colonists. It is esteemed an essential British right that no person shall be subject to any tax but what in person or by his representative he hath a voice in laying.

The British Parliament have many times vindicated this right against the attempts of Kings to invade it. And though perhaps it may be said that the House of Commons, in a large sense, are the representatives of the colonies as well as of the people of Great Britain, yet it is certain that these have no voice in their election. Nor can it be any alleviation of their unhappiness that if this right is taken from them, it is taken by that body who have been the great patrons and defenders of it in the people of Great Britain.

That the colonies have an elected legislature as a lawmaking, tax-laying body is a point we will see again, phrased in different ways, as a component of the American protests.

Besides, the colonies have ever supported a subordinate government among themselves [and] have always been taxed by their own representatives and in their respective legislatures, and have supported an entire domestic government among themselves. Is it just, then, they should be doubly taxed? That they should be obliged to bear the whole charges of their domestic government, and should be as subject to the taxes of the British Parliament as those who have no domestic government to support?

He moves on from the taxation itself to the flawed rationale. "The reason given for this extraordinary taxation?" It was claimed by the British to be the recent war, which "was undertaken for the security of the colonies, and that they ought therefore to be taxed to pay the charge thereby incurred." He offers detailed arguments that the claim "is without foundation." There are other problems with the law, "But to say the truth, it is not only by the taxation itself that the colonists deem themselves aggrieved by the act we are considering."

Thacher then turns to the regulatory aspects of the Sugar Act at great
length.[13] "The knowledge of all the statutes relating to the customs,
of all the prohibitions on exports and imports, and of various intricate cases arising on them, requires a good lawyer." His long discussion ends with, "Much more might be said on these subjects, but I
aim at brevity."

Despite the desire for brevity, he, like Otis, reprises the merchants'
arguments about the economic burden of the duties of the Sugar Act
(e.g., "The duty of three pence a gallon on molasses must entirely
[doom the fishery]"). He asserts that the duties and "effect of the
new regulations" will be that "all the other trade of the colonists
must be at an end." He ridicules the result.

> The exports to the colonies wholly stopped or greatly diminished,
> the demands for those manufactures in Great Britain must be in
> proportion lessened. The substance of those manufacturers, mer-
> chants, and traders whom this demand supports is then gone. . . .
> Doth not this resemble the conduct of the good wife in the fable
> who *killed her hen that every day laid her a golden egg?*[14]

There is a great deal more to this pamphlet, but its importance
for the story of 1764 is that it identifies the Sugar Act as imposing a
tax, the first major essay to make such a specific assertion.

In 1775, John Adams addressed the Sugar Act and Thacher's pamphlet.

> The act of parliament of the 4th George III [i.e., the Sugar Act],
> passed in the year 1764, was the first act of the British parliament
> that ever was passed, in which the design of raising a revenue was
> expressed.

Adams then refers to *The Sentiments of a British American* as
"The first objection to this act."

> Here is a tax, unquestionably external, in the sense in which that
> word is used in the distinction that is made by some between ex-
> ternal and internal taxes, and unquestionably laid in part for the

regulation of trade, yet called a grievance, and a violation of an essential British right, in the year 1764, by one who was then at the head of the popular branch of our constitution, and as well acquainted with the sense of his constituents as any man living. And it is indisputable, that in those words he wrote the almost universal sense of this colony.[15]

AUTUMN IN MASSACHUSETTS

On October 18, Governor Bernard opened the new session of the General Court. Developing and stating the position to be taken by the colony about the Sugar Act and the planned stamp duties was a complex process.

Draft Address to King and Parliament

The assembly prepared a strident protest to recent actions as an address to the king and both houses of Parliament. It was sent to the council for concurrence on October 22, but this did not become the official position of Massachusetts; the council would not concur. I will later discuss the official document resulting from a combined committee, but it is important to first understand the position of the assembly, a draft statement written by Oxenbridge Thacher.

> To the king's most excellent majesty, the right honble Lords spiritual & temporal, & the honble House of Commons in Parliament assembled.
>
> We your Majesty's most loyal & dutifull subjects, the representatives of the province of the Massachusetts bay, beg leave to address your Majesty. . . .

After a long preamble, the petition gets down to business.

> We cannot . . . conceal our grief to find by a late statute [the Sugar Act] such duties laid & regulations established as must not only deprive us of all these resources but . . . *must finally destroy our trade, & as we humbly conceive deprive us of the most essential rights of Britons.*

They make some strictly economic complaints about the Sugar
Act.

> The high Duty on Foreign sugar & molasses must soon distroy
> our Trade to ye Foreign Islands, without which Branch of Com-
> merce our Fisheries must be destroyed, and the many other new
> regulations, introduced or new enforced by the said act, must so
> abridge & discourage our trade as that the province will be utterly
> unable to pay its public debts; whence must soon arise a general
> bankruptcy, and whenever this happens the inhabitants of the
> kingdom of great Britain will, we fear, be great sharers in our
> calamity.

The address then turns to the impending Stamp Act and a discussion of the adverse economic consequences of stamp duties, ending
with "these duties, joined to the other fore mentioned will exhaust
the province of all it's money, and it will be utterly incapable of paying it's public debts."

> But we must further humbly represent to your Majesty *that we
> look upon those duties as a tax*, and which we humbly apprehend
> ought not to be laid without the representatives of the people af-
> fected by them.

The telling phrase "we look upon those duties as a tax" specifically includes, "The high Duty on Foreign sugar & molasses" imposed by the Sugar Act. I call attention to this as a contrast to the
later official petition that does not object to the sugar and molasses
duties as a tax.

> We have learned from the laws of our mother country, and from
> many of the most public & solemn acts; to consider ye rights of
> Britons as sacred & inviolable. And we cannot conceive that the
> colonists have forfeited them by their emigrating a thousand
> leagues, subduing immense forests filled with savage beasts & men
> to the British obedience, protecting at their own expence the
> British subjects at ye great distance from the capital, & thereby

enlarging the British empire & commerce. *Now we have ever supposed this to be one essential right of British subjects, that they shall not be subjected to taxes which, in person or by representative, they have no voice in laying.*

The "essential right" is buttressed by long usage. "In this conclusion we have been fortified by the practice of the English Parliaments in former and later times, which have ever vindicated this right."

Our ancestors & we have been profuse of our blood and treasure in the British cause, and we shall be ever ready to show on every fitting occasion our warm attachment to your Majesty and the nation under your happy government. Nor do we in the least desire that any trade inconsistent with ye real good of the nation should be in the least connived at or favored. But we must & ought to *claim those rights & privileges that being born Britons are inherent to us.*

The close is modest, more-or-less straightforwardly asking for relief without specifying an action. "Wherefore on the whole we humbly pray your Majesty, and your high court of Parliament will be pleased to consider the premises and grant us relief therein."[16]

Petition to the House of Commons

The council objected to the language adopted by the assembly. After lengthy negotiation, the final result was a petition to the House of Commons only, putting forth the official position of Massachusetts about the Sugar Act and the planned stamp duties. Three items stand out: (1) there is no longer any statement of "we look upon those duties as a tax," (2) the protests about the "duties laid" contain no suggestion that they are taxes, but are strictly based on economic principles, and (3) the objection to internal taxes is weak: freedom from internal taxes is a privilege—a revocable privilege—and not a right. In fact, the petition by explicit intent avoids mention of the idea, even the word "right." In addition, the fact of sending the petition only to the House of Commons tends to acknowledge its exclusive authority in this matter.

The first version of the new petition originated in the council and was considered by the assembly on November 1. It was there amended and sent back for concurrence. After further amending, a committee of both chambers chaired by Hutchinson was appointed and an agreement reached. On November 3, 1764, this became the official position of Massachusetts.

> To the Honorable the Commons of Great Britain, in Parliament assembled.
> The petition of the Council and House of Representatives of his Majesty's Province of Massachusetts Bay,
> Most humbly sheweth,
> That the act passed in the last session of Parliament [the Sugar Act] must necessarily *bring many burdens upon the inhabitants* of these colonies & plantations which your petitioners conceive would not have been imposed if a full representation of the state of the colonies had been made to your honourable House.

We see that compared to the draft petition of the assembly, this is going to be a humble pleading rather than a strident claim of right. The weak "bring many burdens upon the inhabitants" sets a different tone than stating the act must "deprive us of the most essential rights of Britons."

> That the duties laid upon foreign sugars & molasses by [the Molasses Act of 1733] if the act had been executed with vigor, must have had the effect of an absolute prohibition.
> That the duties laid on those articles by the present act still remain so great that, however otherwise intended, they must undoubtedly have the same effect.
> That the importation of foreign molasses into this province in particular is of the greatest importance, and a prohibition will be prejudicial to many branches of its trade and will lessen the consumption of the manufactures of Great Britain.

We have seen the following argument (a continuing grievance) in earlier American protests, but this is a particularly thorough explanation of the link between the molasses trade and the maintenance of the fishery.

That if the trade for many years carried on for foreign molasses can be no longer continued, a vent cannot be found for more than one half the fish of inferior quality which is caught & cured by the inhabitants of the province, the French *permitting no fish to be carried by foreigners to any of their islands, unless it be bartered or exchanged for molasses.*

That if there be no sale of fish of inferior quality it will be impossible to continue the fishery; the fish usually sent to Europe will then cost so dear that the French will be able to undersell the English at all the European markets; and by this means one of the most valuable returns to Great Britain will be utterly lost, and that great nursery of seamen destroyed.

A long section follows, pointing out the unjust nature of the new rules about admiralty courts, ending this way.

That the extension of the powers of courts of vice-admiralty has, so far as the jurisdiction of the said courts hath been extended, *deprived the colonies of one of the most valuable of English liberties, trials by juries.*

That every act of Parliament which in this respect *distinguishes his Majesty's subjects in the colonies from their fellow subjects* in Great Britain must create a very sensible concern and grief.

The subject of internal taxes is slowly raised.

That there have been communicated to your petitioners sundry resolutions of the House of Commons in their last session for imposing stamp duties or taxes upon the inhabitants of the colonies, the consideration whereof was referred to the next session.

That your petitioners acknowledge with all gratitude the tenderness of the legislature of Great Britain of the liberties & privileges of the subjects in the colonies, who have always judged by their representatives both of the way & manner in which internal taxes should be raised within their respective governments and of the ability of the inhabitants to pay them.

The following is a weak statement, particularly when compared to the earlier claim by the assembly of "those rights & privileges that being born Britons are inherent to us."

That they humbly hope the colonies in general have so demeaned themselves, more especially during the late war, as *still to deserve the continuance of all those liberties* which they have hitherto enjoyed.

"The inhabitants of this province," between paying for their internal government and the "restraint they are under in their trade for the benefit of Great Britain," are already as "fully burdened as their fellow subjects in Britain."

Your petitioners, therefore, most humbly pray that they may be relieved from the burdens which they have humbly represented to have been brought upon them by the late act of Parliament [and] that the privileges of the colonies relative to *their internal taxes* which they have so long enjoyed may still be continued to them. Signed, S. White, Speaker [of the Assembly]; and A. Oliver, Secretary [to the Council][17]

That the address protests the "duties laid upon foreign sugars & molasses" on economic grounds only implies that such duties are constitutionally acceptable. Even the planned stamp duties almost get a constitutional pass; there is not much objection to the plan to tax the colonies, only a weak hope that their privileges may be continued. A meek protest indeed.

How Was the Petition Developed?
Why was the petition so mild, so meek, so timid? The blunt answer is that Lieutenant Governor Hutchinson browbeat a joint committee into agreeing to his vision of sending to the House of Commons an address that (he thought) could not be considered offensive. The

process of development of the petition explains its nature as a polit-ical decision. Hutchinson dealt with the process in his *History of the Province of Massachusetts Bay.*

> Some days passed in controversy between the two houses, when the difference, at length, was reduced to one word only; which, as it stood in the report, was *privileges*. The house had changed it to *rights*, which the council would not agree to. At length, *liberties* was proposed by the council, and acquiesced in by the house.

The argument over a single word demonstrates the care with which the petition was crafted by the joint committee. Hutchinson goes on that asserting "an exclusive right in the assemblies of the colonies to impose taxes and duties . . . would never be received by the House of Commons." Hutchinson insisted on addressing "the exemption from taxes as an indulgence, which parliament had always shewn to the colonies."[18]

Hutchinson explained the effect of the petition when writing Thomas Pownall in March 1765.

> The proceeding of the general court was also approved and ap-plauded out of doors, until the copy of an address from the as-sembly of New York [the petition of October 18] was brought to Boston by Mr. Bayard, one of the city members This was so high, that the heroes for liberty among us were ashamed of their own conduct and would have recalled what had been done here, if it had not been too late.[19]

The strategy of avoiding a claim of right failed on two fronts: the petition was castigated as an embarrassingly weak statement that failed to protect the rights of the colonists, and it met with no more favor than bold assertions of American rights from other colonies.

Bernard Forwards the Petition

The committee requested the governor to lay "a copy of said petition before his Majesty's ministers." In response, Bernard sent the petition to the Earl of Halifax on November 10.

My Lord,
I hereby enclose to your Lordship a copy of Petition of the Council
and the House of Representatives to the House of Commons of
Great Britain, which I am desired by the said Council and House
of Representatives to lay before his Majesty's Ministers & to beseech the favour of their great influence in behalf of their petition.

He adds his own comments. "It is my Duty to certify my Opinion
upon such extraordinary & intresting occasions. I shall therefore,
with great truth & sincerity, acquaint your Lordship with my Sentiments."

The Heads of the Petition to the House of Commons are these. 1.
*That the Duties upon Melasses are such as will discourage the im-
portation of it & thereby hurt the American fishery*. . . . 6. That
the Trade of America is really the trade of Great Britain, & that
the opening & encouraging it is the most effectual way for Great
Britain to draw money from America.

He offers a number of sentiments keyed to the heads of the petition, but I will present only the first.

I have heretofore considered foreign Melasses as a fund for raising
money: and as such I have been of Opinion that a Duty of [one
penny half penny per gallon] would raise more money than either
a larger or smaller duty.
     But yet I am not so positive as to assert that 2d pr. gallon may
not raise as much or possibly more: but I am persuaded that beyond that the higher the duty the less will be the revenue.

He begins to close.

I have given your Lordship my thoughts upon these subjects with
great regard to truth in my opinion, & have accordingly treated
the Matters with such a freedom as the importance of the Disqui-
sition & my Duty to give your Lordship the best information in
my power required.

His final thought is to credit the lieutenant governor with moderating the October draft petition of the assembly. The expected result? "I am told that these proceedings will be contrasted by those of another province [New York] much to the advantage of this."[20]

HUTCHINSON OPINES ON THE NEW YORK PROTEST

Hutchinson's opinion of the New York protest gives us further insight into his thinking about the way in which Massachusetts presented its petition. The following is a letter to Richard Jackson in the Hutchinson letter book (entered late November) but marked "not sent." He presumably had second thoughts about committing such blunt words to a letter, but they nonetheless reflect his state of mind.

> Since I sent you copy of the petition from this province one of the Representatives of N York has been in town & brot with him copy of the address from the Representatives there. It is said by some Zealots here to be a very spirited performance but really it is the most extraordinary thing I ever saw & not only discovers the authors of it to be unacquainted with all form of proceeding in such cases but that they are strangers to the rules of decency & good manners.[21]

EXPLICIT STATEMENTS

Private correspondence with Mauduit deals more openly with the attitude of the joint committee, and of the assembly, than does the official petition.

"We May Be More Explicit on This Point"

In addition to requesting that Governor Bernard submit the petition, on November 3, the committee sent it to Mauduit, at the same time revealing the rationale for the petition. It states that the Sugar Act "affects this colony more than any other [and] that they have been induced thus to petition [so that] *a decent remonstrance* might procure some relief." They discuss their strategy and then state that freedom from taxation by Parliament is, indeed, a right, not simply a privilege.

We have endeavored to avoid giving offence, and have touched upon our rights in such a manner, as that no inference can be drawn that we have given them up, on the one hand, nor that we set up in opposition to the Parliament, nor deny that we are bound to the observance of acts of Parliament, on the other. *But in a letter to you, we may be more explicit on this point*—a right, the people of the colonies have undoubtedly by charter and commissions to tax themselves. So far as the Parliament shall lay taxes on the colonies, so far they will deprive them of this right.[22]

Reinforcing the More Explicit *Point of View*
On November 12, Cushing wrote Mauduit with elaboration on the committee's letter of November 3.

In their Letter to you they have expressly asserted their exclusive right of Taxing themselves and have endeavored to prove that the Subjects here ought not to be taxed without their Consent either in person [or] by their Representative.

He reinforces that the November 3 petition is couched in political terms.

They have not been *so full and explicit* upon this Head in their Petition least they should give offence to so respectable a Body as they are now applying to, but expect you join with the Other Agents in obtaining leave, if possible, to be heard by Councill [counsel] before the House of Commons upon the subject matter of the Petition, of which this of our Rights is not the least important.
  I understand that the Colonies of New York, Connecticut and Rhode Island, have also remonstrated upon this Occasion. I hope the united sense of the Colonies will have so much weight in this matter as with the united efforts of their respective Agents to obtain for us some relief from the Burdens we already labor under as well as to prevent any additional ones that may be intended.[23]

Even More Explicit

On November 17, Cushing wrote Mauduit again, further expressing the wish, on the part of the assembly, to have been more explicit in the petition of November 3.

> The House of Representatives were clearly for making an ample and full declaration of the exclusive Right of the People of the Colonies to tax themselves and that they ought not to be deprived of a right they had so long enjoyed and which they held by Birth and by Charter; but they could not prevail with the Councill, tho they made several Tryalls, to be more explicit than they have been in the Petition sent you.

He outlines their two alternatives. "Either to join with the Council in the Petition forwarded you by the Secretary, or to petition by themselves," and then details why they chose to join with the Council and accept Hutchinson's political strategy.

> Considering they had wrote you fully upon the matter of Right the last session and had sent you a small tract entitled, *The Rights of the British Colonies* in general [i.e., the Otis memorial] and of the Province of the Massachusetts Bay in particular briefly stated, which they then desired and expected you would make the best use of in your Power, they thought it the less necessary to remonstrate by themselves at this time and therefore upon the whole determined to have the weight of the Council as far as they could, and so concluded to join with them in the present petition tho' not so full as they could have wished.

Cushing states on behalf of the assembly a different posture than the official position of Massachusetts.

> *You will therefore collect the sentiments of the Representative Body of People rather from what they have heretofore sent you than from the present Address.* As the People throughout this Continent are greatly alarmed at this Infringement, as they apprehend, of their most Essential Rights, I hope their Sentiments will have their due weight with the Parliament.[24]

This is a stunning statement, recanting support of the November petition in favor of their earlier stance taken in the letter of June 13.

Although the letter of June 13 is not the official position of Massachusetts, British leaders become aware of it and recognize it as an important statement, perhaps giving a more accurate representation of the position of the colony than the bland official petition.

MORE INSTRUCTIONS

In the final instructions of the year to Jasper Mauduit, Cushing writes on behalf of the assembly on November 28. The long letter, almost another essay, provides further explanation of the economic hardships of the Sugar Act. Its focus is strictly on economic issues and does not dispute the right of Parliament to levy a duty on imports.

> The two Houses in their Petition to the House of Commons have represented, that the Duty laid upon foreign Molasses by the late Act is so high, that it must undoubtedly have the Effect of an absolute Prohibition.

As a consequence, the "whole of the Duties that might be collected" will be small. After rehearsing the arguments of the past twelve months, it makes the usual summary point. Obstructing or prohibiting any American trade "must finally lessen the Trade between Great Britain and her Colonies."

> It must lessen the Ability of the People to pay for British Manufactures; and whatever lessens that Ability, must proportionably lessen the Consumption, and consequently the Importation. From hence it is evident that Great Britain can gain Nothing by the Imposition of Duties and Taxes on her Colonies: For if she does at present, and if it will always be in her Power to draw all their Riches to herself by a Regulation of their Trade, it will be to no Purpose to attempt to get more.[25]

Mauduit made no response to the various and contrary instructions. He received the petition on January 11, 1765, and wrote that he was pleased with the wording, thinking it "a Model or Pattern for all the other Agents to follow and even to join with."

MUTUAL CONGRATULATION

The governor, council, and assembly were all publicly pleased with themselves and their consensus regarding the petition to the House of Commons. On January 10, 1765, Governor Bernard addressed the "Gentlemen of the Council and Gentlemen of the House of Representatives." Regarding the petition, "I flatter myself that these representations will have success, as they must receive great weight from the dutiful manner in which they are formed." The response to the governor came two days later. "We flatter ourselves the representations therein made will have success, not only from the dutiful manner in which they are formed [and so on]."[26]

The self-congratulation was hasty; the political plan to make an inoffensive statement was a failure. The Massachusetts petition was colored in the eyes of Parliament by the June 13 and June 25 letters of the assembly.

RESULT OF THE PETITION TO THE HOUSE OF COMMONS

Richard Jackson was to present the petition, but after seeing others rejected, he chose not to offer that of Massachusetts. The nominal rationale for rejection of petitions was that it was the practice of Parliament not to admit petitions against a money bill; but the real reason was that the House of Commons would not hear any petition that denied the rightful authority of Parliament to impose inland taxes.

The position of the assembly was clear: Parliament has no right to levy either internal taxes or duties for revenue (also a form of taxation). That stance is in stark contrast to the official petition; it prays for relief *only from the economic burdens* of the Sugar Act, with no hint that the molasses duty violates the rights of the colonists. Such a form of protest carried an implication that duties levied for the purpose of revenue are within the authority of Parliament. Even the protest to the impending stamp duty is muted, asking a continuation of privilege. The official position of Massachusetts makes no mention of a violation of the rights of Englishmen, no discussion of a constitutional principle.

Seven

Virginia

V IRGINIA WAS THE LAST OF THE COLONIES TO PREPARE AND DELIVER to king and Parliament its petitions. But its position was defined early by correspondence, instructions to agent Edward Montague, and a pamphlet by Richard Bland that tackled a central issue in the constitutional conflict between Great Britain and the colonies.

LETTER OF RICHARD HENRY LEE

Richard Henry Lee was a wealthy planter who played a major role in Virginia politics and who a decade later introduced the resolution into the Continental Congress "that these United Colonies are, and of right ought to be, free and independent States." In a letter of May 31, 1764, to a friend in London, he expressed the frustration felt by many important men in America.

> Many late determinations of the great, on your side of the water, seem to prove a resolution to oppress North America with the iron hand of power, unrestrained by any sentiment drawn from reason, the liberty of mankind, or the genius of their own government. 'Tis said the House of Commons readily resolved, that it had "a right to tax the subject here, *without the consent of his representative.*" And that, in consequence of this, they had pro-

ceeded to levy on us a considerable annual sum for the support of a body of troops to be kept up in this quarter.

Lee points out "that those brave adventurous Britons, who originally conquered and settled these countries" had expected to live under a free government.

Surely no reasonable being would, at the apparent hazard of his life, quit liberty for slavery; nor could it be just in the benefited, to repay their benefactors with chains instead of the most grateful acknowledgments. And as certain it is that "the free possession of property, the right to be governed by laws made by our representatives, and the illegality of taxation without consent" are such essential principles of the British constitution, that it is a matter of wonder how men, *who have almost imbibed them in their mother's milk*, whose very atmosphere is charged with them, should be of opinion that the people of America were to be taxed without consulting their representatives!

Lee builds on the British constitutional tradition that denies the king any power of taxation, reserving that right to the representatives of the people—in the words of the Bill of Rights, Parliament. But the right of taxation for America does not rest in the body of men under the name *Parliament*, it rests in the *representatives of the people*. For Virginia, the only elected representatives sit in the House of Burgesses.

It will not avail to say that these restrictions on the right of taxation are meant to restrain only the sovereign, and not Parliament. *The intention of the constitution is apparent; to prevent unreasonable impositions on the people*; and no method is so likely to do that as making their own consent necessary for the establishment of such impositions.

The importance of law being made with "their own consent" is central to the prevention of "unreasonable impositions on the people."

But if no such consent is allowed in our case, it will still be an aggravation of our misfortune to be the slaves of five hundred masters instead of one.

He goes on, pointing out unjust violation of "the rights and privileges, to which they are entitled." He ends, "Possibly this step of the mother country," although intended to oppress Americans, instead

> may produce a fatal resentment of parental care being converted into tyrannical usurpation. I hope you will pardon so much on this subject. My mind has been warmed, and I hardly know where to stop.[1]

LETTER OF COMMITTEE OF CORRESPONDENCE

On June 15, the committee of correspondence met to deal with news from agent Edward Montague. (The committee represented the General Assembly—the Council and House of Burgesses—but as a practical matter was under control of the Burgesses.) Montague's letter of March 10 reported the resolutions presented by Grenville the previous day. Although the legislature was not in session, the committee decided on aggressive action.

> Ordered, that Mr. Montague be informed that the Colony is much alarmed at the Attempt in parliament to lay a Duty on the several Commodities mentioned in their Votes . . . particularly on Madeira Wine & the proposal for a Stamp Duty.

(The particular alarm over the duty on Madeira arises from its being a favored beverage of southern aristocrats.)

> That he be desired to oppose this with all his Influence, & as far as he may venture insist on the Injustice of laying any Duties on us, & particularly *taxing the internal Trade* of the Colony without their Consent.

The resulting letter of July 28 states the position of the colony.

We have been very uneasy at an Attempt made in Parliament to lay a Duty on the several Commodities mentioned in their Votes, of which you were pleased to favour us with a Copy; the tax upon Madeira Wine will be very inconvenient to us, & we had it in our Intention to furnish you with such Reasons against it as we thought might have some Weight, but finding from the public Prints that an Act imposing this Duty has already pass'd, it is become unnecessary for us to say any Thing farther upon that Head. The Proposal to lay a stamp Duty . . . is *truly alarming*; [it is a] heavy burthen imposed upon a People already laden with Debts, contracted chiefly in Defence of the Common Cause.

The committee largely ignores the Sugar Act, barely alluding to the duties "on the several Commodities" and finding that on wine to be "inconvenient." Their objection to the proposed stamp duty is more serious.

It may, perhaps, be thought presumptuous in us to attempt or even to desire any Thing which may look like a restraint upon the controlling Power of Parliament.

Nonetheless, they raise the issue of consent.

No Subjects of the King of Great Britain can be justly made subservient to Laws without either their personal Consent, or their Consent by their representatives we take to be the most vital Principle of the British Constitution.

The committee admits Parliament's authority in trade regulation.

It cannot be denied that the Parliament has from Time to Time, where the Trade of the Colonies with other Parts was likely to interfere with that of the Mother Country, made such Laws as were thought sufficient to restrain such Trade to what was judg'd its proper Channel.

But not in internal matters.

But to fix a Tax upon such Part of our Trade & concerns as are merely internal appears to us to be taking a long & hasty Stride & we believe may truly be said to be of the first Importance.

Spotlighting the internal tax (stamp duties) makes a sharp contrast to the lack of protest against customs duties.

We hope it cannot be taken amiss that we, apprehending ourselves so nearly concern'd, should, at least whilst the Matter is in Suspense, humbly represent against it, & take every Measure which the Principles & Laws of our Constitution appear clearly to justify, *to avert a Storm so very replete with the most dangerous Consequences.*

The letter ends with instructions to oppose the upcoming Stamp Act.

We would therefore have you Sir, & do most earnestly recommend to you, as the greatest Object of our present Concern, the exerting your whole weight & Influence so far as Decency will allow in opposing this & every other Measure of the Sort.

The letter was agreed to and signed by members of the committee. "Then Mr. President laid before the Committee a Letter he had rec'd from Mr. Montague since the last Meeting."[2]
Before seeing the committee's action, let's look at that letter of April 11. Montague raises the stakes about stamp duties.

The 15th resolution is the most alarming to the Colonies. The Chancellor of the Exchequer had determined this measure should take place but I informed you in my last of the check we gave to its progress.

Grenville had asserted the right of Parliament to levy *any tax.*

But though he readily acquiesced in postponing this point yet hoped that the *power & sovereignty of parliament over every part of the British dominions for the purpose of raising or collecting any tax* would never be disputed. That if there was a single man doubted it he would take the sense of the House, having heard without doors hints of this nature dropped. *He then called for the sense of Parliament and that the House might not suffer objections of that Nature at a future day.* The Members interested in the Plantations expressed great surprise that a doubt of that nature could ever exist.

Montague then emphasizes how adamant is the House of Commons.

This, to the best of recollection, was all that materially fell from him on the Subject and it appears to me of first importance to the Colonies. The house appeared so unanimous of opinion that America should ease the revenue of this annual expense *that I am persuaded they will not listen to any remonstrance against it.*

He has no advice about what steps the colony should take to avoid the precedent.

I shall only presume to add what appears the determined sense of Government that this money be furnished by America by some means or other; pleas of incapacity will scarce avail and therefore I should conceive it would be extreme worthy of your serious attention what may be the consequence of introducing such a *precedent as the imposition of a Stamp Tax* by British Parliament.[3]

The response to the April letter was not sent off to a committee, but rather, "This P. S. was immediately penned at the Table."

Since writing the foregoing Part of this Letter, we have received your last of 11 April. Every Mention of the parliament's Intention to lay an Inland Duty upon us gives us fresh Apprehension of the fatal Consequences that may arise to Posterity from such a precedent; but we doubt not that the Wisdom of a British parliament will lead them to distinguish between a Power and Right to do any act.[4]

At the end, they direct Montague to seek a postponement to the next meeting of the General Assembly on October 30.

RICHARD BLAND: THE COLONEL DISMOUNTED

In August, Richard Bland published a pamphlet, *The Colonel Dismounted . . . Containing a Dissertation upon the Constitution of the Colony*. Bland was one of the leading citizens of Virginia and an influential member of the House of Burgesses. The pamphlet was inspired by events outside our story and was written in late 1763. Bland chose to publish it at this time because the essay advances ideas relevant to the current controversy, particularly related to legislative authority.

Bland is the first essayist to deal directly with the division of authority between the colonial legislature and Parliament. Bland addresses the division of authority by making a distinction between *internal and external government*, allocating authority, respectively, to the colonies and to Parliament. The distinction will help place limits on the authority of Parliament and clarify aspects of the coming struggle for legislative power.

It is his intent "to examine into the power of the General Assembly to enact laws." The examination starts by pointing out that Virginians are Englishmen, implicitly holding the rights of Englishmen.

> I do not suppose, Sir, that you look upon the present inhabitants of Virginia as a people conquered by the British arms. If indeed we are to be considered only as the savage aborigines of this part of America, we cannot pretend to the rights of English subjects; but if we are the descendants of Englishmen, who by their own consent and at the expense of their own blood and treasure undertook to settle this new region for the benefit and aggrandizement of the parent kingdom, the native privileges our progenitors enjoyed must be derived to us from them.

He ends with this observation: the rights "could not be forfeited by their migration to America." He starts a chain of logic—premise and deduction: given *this*, then therefore *that*. Everything else depends on this idea.

Under an English government all men are born free, are *only subject to laws made with their own consent*, and cannot be deprived of the benefit of these laws without a transgression of them.

Now we are at the central point of the essay: the distinction in government *spheres of authority*.

If then the people of this colony are free born, and have a right to the liberties and privileges of English Subjects, they must necessarily have a legal constitution, that is, a legislature, composed in part, of the representatives of the people, who may enact laws for the *INTERNAL government* of the colony, and suitable to its various circumstances and occasions; and without such a representative, I am bold enough to say, no law can be made.

Bland defines internal government in terms of the power or authority of the legislature of the colony. He first establishes what the legislature cannot do.

By the term INTERNAL government, it may be easily perceived that I exclude from the legislature of the colony all power derogatory to their dependence upon the mother kingdom; for as we cannot lose the Rights of Englishmen by our removal to this continent, so neither can we withdraw our dependence without destroying the constitution.

The definition is advanced by his next assertion; it states the authority of Parliament, but by doing so it imposes a limitation.

In every instance, therefore, of our EXTERNAL government, we are, and must be subject to the authority of the British Parliament, but in no others. For if the Parliament should impose laws upon us merely relative to our INTERNAL government, it deprives us, as far as those laws extend, of the most valuable part of our birthright as Englishmen, of being governed by laws made with our own consent.

So he gives full authority in the internal sphere of government to the legislature of the colony. He continues to build on the internal/external model to further establish a boundary to the rightful authority of Parliament.

> As all power, therefore, is excluded from the colony of withdrawing its dependence from the mother kingdom, so is all power over the colony excluded from the mother kingdom but such as respects its EXTERNAL government. I do not deny but that the Parliament, as the stronger power, can force any laws it shall think fit upon us, but the inquiry is not what it can do, but what constitutional right it has to do so. And *if it has not* any constitutional right, *then any tax* respecting our INTERNAL polity which may hereafter be imposed on us by act of Parliament is arbitrary, as depriving us of our rights, *and may be opposed.*

Based on the above analysis, he makes this expansive declaration of the authority of a colonial legislature.

> From these principles, which I take to be incontrovertible, as they are deduced from the nature of the English constitution, it is evident that the *legislature of the colony have a right to enact any law they shall think necessary* for their INTERNAL government.

He next desires to "examine the power the General Assembly derives from grants from the crown, abstracted from the original rights of the people."

> King James I by his charter, under the great seal of England, granted the dominion of Virginia to the Treasurer and Company of Adventurers, and gave them full power and authority to constitute a form of government in the colony as near as might be agreeable to the government and policy of England.
>   Pursuant to this power, the Treasurer and Company by their charter established the legislature in the governor, Council, and representatives of the people, to be called the General Assembly, with "free power to treat, consult, and conclude as well of all

emergent occasions concerning the public weal of the colony and every part thereof, as *also to make, ordain, and enact such general laws and orders* for the behoof of the colony and the good government thereof as shall from time to time appear necessary or requisite."

And the authority has continued. "The General Assemblies have continued to exercise this legislative power from that time."

From this short review of our constitution, it may be observed that the people have an original right to a legal government [and] that this right has been confirmed to them by charter, which establishes the General Assembly with a general power [to make laws, etc.]. Which power, by a *constant and uninterrupted usage and custom*, they have continued to exercise for more than 140 years.

His invocation of usage and custom is significant. The British constitution being unwritten, those aspects of government that have long prevailed without objection become part of the constitution. He quotes the famous jurist Lord Coke.

"Where the King by charter or letters patent grants to a country the laws of England or a power to make laws for themselves, [neither] he nor his successors can alter or abrogate the same."

Despite Bland's aggressive defense of the authority of the General Assembly, he emphasizes respect for authority, balanced by broader duties. A citizen should hold

a high reverence for the majesty of the King's authority, and shall upon every occasion yield a due obedience to all its just powers and prerogatives; but submission, even to the supreme magistrate, *is not the whole duty of a citizen,* especially such a submission as he himself does not require: *something is likewise due to the rights of our country, and to the Liberties of Mankind.*[5]

To amplify Bland's assertion about having, "a right to enact any law they shall think necessary for their INTERNAL government," it is worth adding that in March 1766, he published a sequel, *An Inquiry into the Rights of the British Colonies*. He moved further down the path he started in 1764, being explicit that each colony "had a regular Government long before the first Act of Navigation, and were respected as a distinct State, independent, *as to their internal Government,* of the original Kingdom, but united with her, as to their external Polity."[6]

Although Bland does not define exactly what he means by internal and external government, it is clear "that Parliament's authority—to legislate as well as to tax—stopped short of the Atlantic coast of the colonies and did not extend over any affair relating exclusively to the internal life of the colonies."[7]

NOVEMBER RESOLUTIONS

The House of Burgesses met on October 30. Speaker John Robinson introduced the Massachusetts letter of June 25 (to which Virginia later responded in favorable terms). On November 14, the House approved resolves that provide insight into the attitude of the Virginians. They direct that petitions be drawn up to the king, Lords, and Commons.

First, the king.

Resolved, That a most humble and dutiful Address be presented to his Majesty, imploring his Royal Protection of . . . their natural and civil Rights as men and as Descendants of Britons; *which Rights must be violated if Laws, respecting the internal government, and Taxation* of themselves, are imposed upon them by any other Power than that derived from their own Consent, by and with the Approbation of their Sovereign, or his Substitute.

Second, the Lords.

Resolved, That a Memorial be prepared to be laid before the Right Hon. the Lords Spiritual and Temporal in Parliament assembled, intreating their Lordships, by a proper and reasonable Interposition and Exertion of their Power, not to suffer the People of this Colony to be enslaved or oppressed by Laws respecting their *internal* Polity, and Taxes imposed on them in a Manner that is unconstitutional.

And third, the Commons.

Resolved, That a Memorial be prepared to be laid before the Honourable the House of Commons, to assert, with decent Freedom, the Rights and Liberties of the People of this Colony as British Subjects, to remonstrate that Laws for their internal Government, or Taxation, *ought not to be imposed by any Power but what is delegated to their Representatives*, chosen by themselves. [Taxation by Parliament would be] a Violation of the most sacred and valuable Principle of the Constitution.[8]

(The Burgesses eventually prepared a remonstrance, an assertive form of a memorial.)

DECEMBER PETITIONS

The three petitions were drawn up by the Burgesses, and approved by the General Assembly on December 18. Of great significance compared to those of Massachusetts, the petitions received concurrence from the Crown-appointed Council. Although still bold and direct, the original drafts had been amended, made less strident, in order to obtain that concurrence.

The influence of Bland's thinking is evident throughout the Virginia petitions. The use of the phrase *internal polity* (meaning Bland's internal government) expands the arena of protest beyond the threat of internal taxation: they question the supremacy and authority of Parliament. Thomas Jefferson, writing in a reflective mood fifty years later, referred to these writings as "the famous address to the king and memorials to the Houses of Lords and Commons, on the proposal of the Stamp Act."

Address to the King

To the King's Most Excellent Majesty:
Most Gracious Sovereign,

After the usual assurances of "firm and inviolable attachment," the address goes on

> to intreat that your Majesty will be graciously pleased to protect your People of this Colony in the Enjoyment of their *ancient and inestimable Right of being governed by such Laws respecting their internal Polity and Taxation as are derived from their own Consent.*
>
> [This is] a Right which as Men, and Descendants of *Britons, they have ever quietly possessed* since first by Royal Permission and Encouragement they left the Mother Kingdom to extend its Commerce and Dominion.

The right is not recent; it rests on custom and precedent, and has been long recognized.

> Your Majesty's dutiful Subjects of Virginia most humbly and unanimously *hope that this invaluable Birthright,* descended to them from their Ancestors, and in which they have been protected by your Royal Predecessors, will not be suffered to receive an Injury under the Reign of your Sacred Majesty, already so illustriously distinguished by your gracious Attention to the Liberties of the People.

The apparent servile nature of the "hope" is just boilerplate for the king. In fact, the Virginians will not suffer their rights to be abridged.

Memorial to the Lords

> To the Right Honourable the Lords Spiritual and Temporal, in Parliament Assembled:
> The Memorial of the Council and Burgesses of Virginia now met in General Assembly,
> Humbly Represents,
> That your Memorialists hope on Application to your Lordships, the fixed and hereditary Guardians of British Liberty, will not be thought improper at this Time, when Measures are proposed sub-

versive, as they conceive, of that Freedom which all Men, especially those who derive their Constitution from Britain, have a Right to enjoy.

They express the basic idea of no taxation without representation.

Your Memorialists conceive it to be a fundamental Principle of the British constitution, without which Freedom can nowhere exist, that the *People are not subject to any Taxes but such as are laid on them by their own Consent, or by those who are legally appointed to represent them.*

This next point—about representatives being affected by the taxes they levy—is crucial.

Property must become too precarious for the Genius of a free People which can be taken from them at the Will of others, who cannot know what Taxes such People can bear, or the easiest Mode of raising them; and who are not under that Restraint, which is the greatest Security against a burthensome Taxation, *when the Representatives themselves must be affected by every Tax imposed on the People.*

Neither members of Parliament nor their constituents are adversely affected by taxes imposed upon Americans.

Your Memorialists are therefore led into an humble Confidence that your Lordships will not think any Reason sufficient to support such a Power in the British Parliament, where the Colonies *cannot be represented*; a Power never before constitutionally assumed, and which if they have a Right to exercise on any Occasion must necessarily establish this melancholy Truth, that the Inhabitants of the Colonies are the Slaves of Britons, from whom they are descended.

When the king needed aid to support imperial activity (for example, during the recent Seven Years' War), there was no levy of taxes.

Instead,

> Your Memorialists have been invested with the Right of taxing their own People *from the first Establishment of a regular Government in the Colony,* and Requisitions have been constantly made to them by their Sovereigns on all Occasions when the Assistance of the Colony was thought necessary to preserve the British Interest in America.

Such a procedure of making requisitions had established a precedent—what the Americans now see as the proper constitutional procedure—for raising revenue from the colonies. The point is that they tax "their own People" to fulfill the revenue requested by the sovereign. The Burgesses are building up to a claim that taxes are unnecessary and unconstitutional. The memorial phrases it this way.

> They must conclude they cannot now be deprived of a Right they have so long enjoyed, and which they have never forfeited.

Anyway, there is no need to tax Virginia; it has contributed its share of expenses, has fulfilled the requisitions.

> The Expenses incurred during the last War, in *Compliance with the Demands* on this Colony by our late and present most gracious Sovereigns, have involved us in a Debt of near Half a Million; a Debt not likely to decrease under the continued Expense we are at in providing for the Security of the People against the Incursions of our savage Neighbors . . . and the late Restrictions upon the Trade of the Colonies render the Circumstances of the People extremely distressful, and which, if Taxes are accumulated upon them by the British Parliament, will make them truly deplorable.

There we see a mild nod toward the distress of "late Restrictions," meaning the Sugar Act. But there is no constitutional objection. They continue to assert exclusive authority over taxation.

Your Memorialists cannot suggest to themselves any Reason why they should not still be trusted with the Property of their People, with whose Abilities, and the least burthensome Mode of taxing (with great Deference to the superior Wisdom of Parliament) they must be best acquainted.

They close with affirmation of "the purest Loyalty and Affection." At the very end they make a modest request. "They do most humbly pray your Lordships to take this Subject into your Consideration with the Attention that is due to the Well being of the Colonies."

Remonstrance to the Commons

The boldest of the petitions was that of the remonstrance to the House of Commons, largely from the pen of George Wythe, one of the leading patriots of Virginia. Jefferson said of Wythe that "his virtue was of the purest tint; his integrity inflexible, and his justice exact."

To the Honourable the Knights, Citizens, and Burgesses of Great Britain, in Parliament assembled:
The Remonstrance of the Council and Burgesses of Virginia.

Here is the problem seen by the Burgesses. The House of Commons had resolved

That towards defending, protecting, and securing the British Colonies and Plantations in America, *it may be proper to charge certain Stamp Duties in the said Colonies and Plantations.*

And "that the same Subject, which was then declined, may be resumed and further pursued in a succeeding Session."

The Council and Burgesses of Virginia, met in General Assembly, judge it their indispensable Duty, in a respectful Manner, but with decent Firmness, to remonstrate against such a Measure.

They express the wish that "a Cession of those Rights, which in their Opinion must be infringed by that Procedure, may not be inferred from their Silence, at so important a Crisis." Here is made clear the nature of representation, implicitly denying the authority of Parliament.

> They conceive it is essential to British Liberty that Laws imposing Taxes on the People ought not to be made without the Consent of Representatives chosen by themselves; who, at the same Time that they are acquainted with the Circumstances of their Constituents, *sustain a Proportion of the Burthen laid on them.*

The Burgesses turn to promises made long ago, as a grant, a license, given by the Crown of England, in order to encourage establishment of the colony.

> This Privilege, inherent in the Persons who discovered and settled these Regions, *could not be renounced or forfeited by their Removal hither*, not as Vagabonds or Fugitives, but licensed and encouraged by their Prince and animated with a laudable Desire of enlarging the British Dominion, and extending its Commerce.

Although Virginia is at this time no longer a charter colony, the essential features of its old charter (as referred to by Bland) have been incorporated into royal commissions that have been stable for many years.

> On the contrary, it was secured to them and their Descendants, with all other Rights and Immunities of British Subjects, by a Royal Charter, which hath been invariably recognized and confirmed by his Majesty and his Predecessors in their *Commissions to the several Governours*, granting a Power, and prescribing a Form of Legislation; according to which, Laws for the Administration of Justice, and for the Welfare and good Government of the Colony, have been hitherto enacted by the Governour, Council, and General Assembly, and to them Requisitions and Applications for Supplies have been directed by the Crown.

The Burgesses give specific examples in "which former sovereigns entertained of these rights and privileges." They conclude that because of such precedents, "the Remonstrants do not discern by what Distinction they can be deprived of that sacred Birthright and most valuable Inheritance by their Fellow Subjects." And, reaching the immediate situation of stamp duties, they further do not discern "with what Propriety they can be taxed or affected in their Estates by the Parliament, wherein they are not, and indeed cannot, constitutionally be represented."

The ending shows a mix of respect and firm conviction, balancing a soft phrase with a hard one.

> From these Considerations, *it is hoped that* the Honourable House of Commons will not prosecute a Measure which those who may suffer under it cannot but look upon as fitter for Exiles driven from their native Country.

After that hope, they boldly announce that

> Patriots *will never consent* to the Exercise of anti-constitutional Power, which even in this remote Corner may be dangerous in its Example to the interiour Parts of the British Empire, and will certainly be detrimental to its Commerce.[9]

FORWARDING THE PETITIONS

On December 20, the committee of correspondence sent the documents to Montague. It provided unusually detailed direction. "We must desire you to try every possible method of having them properly presented and use your utmost Influence in supporting them."

> We are under some apprehensions that you will meet with Difficulty in getting the memorial to the Commons laid before them, as we have heard of their refusing to receive Petitions from the Colonies in former similar Instances.

(In fact, refusal to hear petitions against proposed acts of revenue—money bills—was the usual practice of the House of Commons.)

If this should be now the case we think you should have them printed and dispersed over the Nation, or the substance of them at least published in such manner as you may think least liable to objection, that the People of England may be acquainted with the Privileges & Liberties we claim as British Subjects; as their Brethren and the dreadful apprehensions we are under of being deprived of them in the unconstitutional method proposed.

The committee members continue to demonstrate confidence in the support and cooperation of the other colonies. "We are persuaded you will be heartily seconded by the Agents for the other American Colonies."[10]

On December 24, Lieutenant Governor Francis Fauquier gave the Board of Trade his opinion about the petitions.

I am informed they [the Council and Burgesses] have *jointly ordered* an address to His Majesty and a memorial to the House of Peers, with another to the House of Commons, to their Agent, to be by him promptly recommended to be presented as directed.

In the resolutions of the House of Burgesses *the terms are very warm and indecent* as Your Lordships will observe in their Journals; but I have been told by some Gentlemen of the Committee appointed to draw them up, that their whole study has been to endeavour to mollify them, and they have reason to hope there is nothing now in them which will give the least offence.

It is clear that Fauquier understood the petitions to be the product of the Burgesses and was aware of the negotiation and revisions that went on to make them acceptable to the Council. He explains, "I thought it my duty to give your Lordships the most early intelligence of this matter in my power."

I have not yet seen them, but when they are fairly transcribed and the dispatches made up for their Agent, I apprehend they will be communicated to me, as all other dispatches are. The Subject matter of them is praying to be permitted to tax themselves.[11]

RESULT OF THE PETITION TO THE HOUSE OF COMMONS

Montague could find no member of the House of Commons willing to present the aggressive Virginia remonstrance. Even after being toned down in committee, it was still viewed as denying the authority of Parliament. He devised by himself a more modest petition in order to find a sponsor.

The petition was the first of several offered to the House and hence occasioned the most debate. The best story about what occurred comes not from Montague but from Charles Garth, agent for South Carolina and a member of the House of Commons, writing about the treatment of the petitions by the House on February 15, 1765.

> Sir William Meredith offered a petition from the agents of Virginia against the said bill, the subject matter of which he stated in his place, and mov'd for leave to bring it up; I seconded the motion, thereupon a debate arose whether to receive or reject it; the arguments for rejecting were founded on the usage and practice of Parliament for the last 30 years.

Garth confirms that the policy was "unquestion'd not to admit petitions against a Money Bill." But there was more than a simple question of procedure. "This was not the sole reason that determin'd the fate of the petitions that were offer'd." Here is the real rationale for rejecting the petitions.

> The House declared they would not suffer a petition that should hint at *questioning the supremacy and authority of Parliament to impose taxes* in every part of the British Dominions. The debate ended with the question put for leave to bring up the petition, which was carry'd in the negative. Some of the petitions that were framed in America and sent over from some of the Colonies to their agents questioned the power of Parliament in very high tones.[12]

The December petitions were the last of the American protests of 1764 and provided a framework for the American protests of 1765 and later years.

A dramatic illustration of the enduring effect of these arguments is provided by Virginia itself when—only five months later, after the Stamp Act had been passed despite the American protests of 1764— the Burgesses made the now-famous *Stamp Act Resolves* (introduced by Patrick Henry in May 1765). Those resolutions sparked the American protests of that year. This resolve summed up the exclusive right of taxation.

> Resolved, that his Majesty's liege People of this his most ancient and loyal Colony, have without Interruption *enjoyed the inestimable Right of being governed by such Laws respecting their internal Polity and Taxation as are derived from their own Consent.*[13]

It is easy to see how that 1765 resolve is modeled, in concept and phrasing, on the December 1764 address to the king, beseeching him to "protect your people of this Colony"

> in the *Enjoyment of their ancient and inestimable Right of being governed by such Laws respecting their internal Polity and Taxation as are derived from their own Consent.*

Eight

Connecticut

THE CONNECTICUT PROTEST CONSISTED OF AN ESSAY, LARGELY prepared by Governor Thomas Fitch, that was also the major part of a petition to the House of Commons.

LEGISLATIVE ACTION IN MAY

When the Connecticut General Assembly met on May 10, Fitch submitted for its consideration a letter of March 10 from agent Richard Jackson that informed the colony about Grenville's March resolutions. The assembly appointed Fitch, assisted by Ebenezer Silliman, George Wyllys, and Jared Ingersoll,[1] "to collect and set in the most advantageous light all such arguments and objections as may justly and reasonably [be] advanced against creating and collecting a revenue in America, more particularly in this Colony, and especially against effecting the same by Stamp Duties."[2]

GOVERNOR THOMAS FITCH: REASONS WHY . . .

The result was an essay published as a pamphlet approved by the assembly in October: *Reasons why the British Colonies in America should not be charged with Internal Taxes.* The essay did a good job of dealing with the stamp duties but was not much of an argument against the broader issue of "collecting a revenue in America." The pamphlet, along with the one by Richard Bland, is one of the early American essays to address a central constitutional issue: how can authority be divided between Parliament and the legislature of a subordinate government? Fitch, like Bland, strives to make a distinction between internal and external government—spheres of government authority.

The essay denies Parliament the right to tax the colonies. (I should explain that the only impositions seen as taxes by Fitch are internal taxes. He does not use the phrase *external tax*.) Of greater importance is what Fitch concedes: that Parliament has an unrestricted right to impose duties in order to draw revenue from the colonies. Fitch makes the specific determination that duties for revenue (he will not call them taxes) are within the external sphere of government and therefore within the authority of Parliament. He starts out by discussing the rights of subjects in the realm, those who are represented in Parliament.

> By the Constitution, Government, and Laws of Great Britain, the English are a Free People. Their Freedom consists principally if not wholly in this general Privilege, that "NO LAWS CAN BE MADE OR ABROGATED, WITHOUT THEIR CONSENT, BY THEIR REPRESENTATIVES IN PARLIAMENT."

Reference to "consent, by their *representatives in Parliament*" makes this an empty privilege for the Americans, having no representatives in Parliament.

> By the *Common Law of England*, every Commoner hath a Right not to be subjected to Laws made without his Consent, and because such Consent (by Reason of the great Inconvenience and Confusion attending Numbers, in such Transactions) cannot be given by every individual Man in Person, therefore is the Power of rendering such Consent, lodged in the Hands of Representatives, by them elected and chosen for that Purpose. Their Subjection, then, to their Laws, is not forced, but voluntary.

This is another statement of the "right of representation." It is by this common-law right that there must be "no taxation without representation."

For if the Privilege of not being taxed without their Consent, be once taken from them, Liberty and Freedom are certainly gone with it. *That Power which can tax as it shall think proper, may govern as it pleases; and those subjected to such Taxations and Government, must be far, very far from being a free People.* They cannot, indeed, be said to enjoy even so much as the Shadow of English Liberties.

Now we see a turning point as he moves to discuss the situation in America.

Upon these general and fundamental Principles, it is conceived that the Parliament . . . *doth not extend its Taxations to such Parts of the British Dominions, as are not represented in that grand Legislature of the Nation.*

He starts six numbered considerations.

First. The People in the Colonies and Plantations in America are really, truly, and in every Respect, as much the King's Subjects, as those born and living in Great Britain are.

And they therefore owe "an inseparable Allegiance to the King."

Secondly. All the King's Subjects, both in Great Britain and in the Colonies and Plantations in America, have Right to the same general and essential Privileges of the British Constitution, or those Privileges which denominate them to be a free People.

He goes on, finally coming to this.

It therefore seems apparent that the King's Subjects in the Plantations have a Right, and that it is for the Honour of the Crown and the Law, that they should have a Right, to the general and essential Privileges of the British Constitution, as well as the rest of their Fellow-Subjects.

Then he quotes from the still-valid Connecticut charter of 1662, saying the king does

"Ordain, Declare and Grant, unto the said Governor and Company . . . and every of their Children . . . all Liberties and Immunities of free and natural Subjects . . . as if they, and every of them, were born within the Realm of England."

Fitch believes, as do all American leaders, that the charter is not merely a grant but is a "Declaration and Confirmation" of existing rights. They are "declarative of the Principles of the ancient Common Law of England, and of the common *Rights of Englishmen*."

Thirdly. In order that the King's Subjects in the Colonies and Plantations in America might have and enjoy the like Liberties and Immunities as other of their Fellow-Subjects are favoured with, it was and is necessary the *Colonies should be vested with the Authority and Power of Legislation*; and this they have accordingly assumed and exercised, from their first regular Settlement, down to this Time.

He returns to a major theme of law being made only "by their representatives." He is now talking about America, therefore does not conclude "in Parliament."

It is a clear Point that the Colonies may not, they cannot, be represented in Parliament; and if they are not vested with legislative Authority within themselves, where they may be represented by Persons of their own electing, it is plain they will not be represented in any Legislature at all, and, consequently, if they are subjected to any Laws, it must be to such as they have never consented to either by themselves or any Representatives, which will be directly contrary to that before-mentioned fundamental Principle of the British constitution, that "NO LAWS CAN BE MADE OR ABROGATED, WITHOUT THE CONSENT OF THE PEOPLE, BY THEIR REPRESENTATIVES."

The charter is clear that, "A full Power of Legislation is granted to the Colony." The power is further supported by the British constitution, and by usage, by custom. Their exclusive authority for taxation has for a long time been agreed to by king and Parliament.

> And these Powers, Rights and Privileges the Colony has been in Possession of for more than a Century past. *This Power of Legislation necessarily includes in it an Authority to impose Taxes. . . .* These Privileges and Immunities, these Powers and Authorities, the Colony claims, not only in Virtue of their Right to the general Principles of the British Constitution, and by Force of the Royal Declaration and Grant in their Favour, but also as having been in the Possession, Enjoyment and Exercise of them for so long a Time, and constantly owned, acknowledged and allowed to be just in the Claim and Use thereof, by the Crown, the Ministry, and the Parliament.

He eventually comes to the purpose of the pamphlet: argue against stamp duties.

> *Fourthly.* That charging Stamp Duties or other internal Taxes on the Colonies in America by parliamentary Authority will be an Infringement of the aforementioned Rights and Privileges, and deprive the Colonists of their Freedom and Inheritance
>
> If these internal Taxations take Place, and the Principles upon which they must be founded are adopted and carried into Execution, the Colonies will have no more than a Shew of Legislation left, nor the King's Subjects in them any more than the Shadow of true English Liberty.

It is not only an initial tax that would be a problem.

> The same Principles which will justify such a Tax of a Penny, will warrant a Tax of a Pound, an hundred, or a thousand Pounds, and so on without Limitation; and if they will warrant a Tax on one Article, they will support one on as many Particulars as shall be thought necessary to raise any Sum proposed.

As part of his continued discussion of the fourth consideration, he answers a potential objection.

OBJECTION

Perhaps it may be here objected that these Principles, if allowed, *will prove too much* [and hence deny that Parliament] has a Superintendency over all the Colonies and Plantations abroad, and Right to govern and controul them as shall be thought best.

The idea of "prove too much" is a hot-button issue; some British officials later charge that yielding on taxes would soon lead to American demands to repeal the laws of trade.

ANSWER

To Objections and Observations of this Kind it may be answered, that as the Parliament of Great Britain is most certainly vested with the supreme Authority of the Nation, and its Jurisdiction and Power most capacious and transcendent, the Colonies will be far, very far from urging or even attempting any Thing in Derogation of the Power or Authority of that august Assembly, or pretending to prescribe Bounds or Limits to the Exercise of their Dominion.

He is explicit that Parliament has authority to make some sorts of law without popular approval, law that affects Americans.

Nothing in the foregoing Observations, be sure, is intended by way of Objection, but that the Crown by its Prerogative, or the Parliament by its supreme and general Jurisdiction, may justly order and do some Things which may affect the Property of the American Subjects in a Way which, *in some Sense*, may be said to be independent upon or *without the Will or Consent of the People*, as by Regulations of Trade and Commerce and the like; and by general Orders relative to and Restrictions of their Conduct for the Good of the Whole.

This is a direct contradiction to his earlier assertion that *no laws can be made* "without the consent of the people by their representatives." But the reasoning is muddy, obscure; he throws in the phrase "in some Sense." How does he reach this conclusion? Because trade regulation, including duties, is in the external sphere of government.

At this point he begins his justification for Parliament's rightful authority to establish duties on trade, even for the purpose of revenue. Such a duty is not a tax.

> For as the Colonies are so many Governments independent of each other, or not subjected the one to the other, they can only establish Regulations within and for themselves respectively; and as they are all subordinate to and dependent upon the Mother Country . . . it becomes plainly expedient that there should be some *supreme Director over all His Majesty's Dominions*; and this Character and Authority, all Men must acknowledge and allow, properly belong to the *British Parliament*.

He gives all control over trade to Parliament, and then transforms trade regulation into unfettered levy of duties.

> It is humbly conceived, that the Subjects in the Colonies may enjoy their Rights, Privileges and Properties, as Englishmen, and yet, for political Reasons, be restrained from some particular Correspondence or Branches of Trade and Commerce, or may be subjected therein to such Duties, Charges and Regulations as the *supreme Power may judge proper* to establish as so many Conditions of enjoying such Trade. Reasons of State may render it expedient to prohibit some Branches of Trade and to burden others as aforesaid.

More directly: Parliament may not levy taxes; Parliament can, as judged proper, levy duties and charges on trade. Here is his rationale.

> Such Regulations will doubtless appear, upon Examination, rather to be a preventing the Subject from acquiring Property, than taking it from him, after it is legally become his own.
>
> What therefore is designed to be urged from these general Principles of the British Constitution, is, that the Legislatures of the

Colonies ought to be left entire, and that His Majesty's good Subjects in them should be permitted the continued Enjoyment of
their essential Rights, Immunities and Privileges, which will not,
as is supposed, by any Means be the Case, if the internal Taxations
before mentioned should take Place.

Parliament has a role in external government: restrictions and regulations.

But if Restrictions on Navigation, Commerce, or other external
Regulations only are established, the internal Government, Powers
of taxing for its Support, an Exemption from being taxed without
Consent, and other Immunities, which legally belong to the Subjects of each Colony, agreeable to their own particular Constitutions, will be and continue in the Substance of them whole and
entire; Life, Liberty and Property, in the True use of the Terms,
will then remain secure and untouched.

He returns to the specific issue.

Fifthly. Another Reason offered as an objection against charging
Stamp Duties, &c in the Colonies, may be drawn from the Consequence of such a Measure, as it is most probable, if not certain,
it will, in the Event, prove prejudicial to Great Britain itself.

The rationale is elaboration of the standard American argument
that the more the colonies prosper, "the greater will be the Advantage
not only to them but also to the Nation at Home."

Sixthly. Furthermore to [reinforce the objections, consider the]
special Services and Circumstances of the Colony of Connecticut.

As do many of the colonial writings, Fitch goes on (page after
page) elaborating on the importance of the colony to the mother
country. But finally, in answer to the following objection, he gets to
a key section of the essay, making concrete his acceptance of duties
for revenue.

OBJECTION
Perhaps, after all that hath been offered, it will be objected by some that America ought, and is able to bear a just Proportion of the American Expence; and that as the Duty already charged will, they suppose, not be sufficient to defray that Expence, it becomes necessary to make Additions to the Duties already laid.

In the answer below, Hopkins responds that both the amount necessary for the expense and the proper contribution of America is "uncertain and difficult to determine." But in any event the contribution should not be "done in a Way that shall be an Infringement on the Constitutions of the Colonies."

ANSWER
Therefore whatever may be done in this Matter, it is humbly trusted will surely be effected in such Manner as to *leave the Legislatures of the Colonies entire, and the People in the full Possession and Enjoyment of their just Rights and Immunities.* This, it is conceived, might be effected by a Duty (if thought necessary and proper) on the Importation of Negroes, and [export duties] on the Fur Trade, etc.; for although that on Slaves may and doubtless will fall with most Weight where the greatest Numbers are imported, yet will none be charged thereby but such as voluntarily submit to it.

This presents in sharp relief the distinction between external customs duties, fully accepted as being within the authority of Parliament, as contrasted with the internal taxes that should not be charged. It is noteworthy that the "Additions to the Duties" he suggests are intended to raise revenue to defray the American expense. He makes no pretense that the duties are to regulate trade. In sum, if additional revenue is needed from the colonies, Parliament should impose duties on trade and not internal taxes. (It is no surprise that the duties he suggests would have no adverse effect on Connecticut.)[3]

After finishing with the six considerations, he moves to closing ideas that address broader, more general issues. First, a long premise.

Having thus shewn that the English are a free People; that their Freedom consists in these general privileges, that no laws can be made or abrogated without their consent by representatives, and for that purpose have right to elect their representatives [etc.].

Therefore

The colonies and plantations in America, according to the general principles of the national constitution, are vested with authority of legislation and have right to be represented in their assemblies, in whom that authority is lodged, and with whose consent they are to be governed by the Crown . . .

The sentence rambles on for another hundred words or so with the same idea, but finally comes to this conclusion.

[C]*harging stamp duties, or internal taxes on the colony, by authority of Parliament, will be inconsistent with those authorities and privileges* which the colonies and the people in them legally enjoy, and have, with the approbation of the supreme power of the nation, been in the use and possession of for a long course of years.

At the end, the essay has the flavor of a petition.

It is now concluded that on account of these and such other weighty reasons as may occur, a British Parliament, whose design is to keep up that constitution, support the honor and prerogative of the Crown, and maintain the privileges of the people, will have a tender regard for the rights and immunities of the King's subjects in the American colonies and *charge no internal taxations upon them without their consent*.[4]

Fundamental to Fitch's reasoning is that any tax is an internal tax. And he refuses to recognize any right or authority of Parliament to levy taxes. He does not recognize or use the phrase "external tax." A duty for raising revenue is not an external tax; it is just a duty. This pamphlet puts Connecticut firmly in the camp of those who have no constitutional objection to impositions stated as port duties. The assembly sent the essay to Jackson in October with the admonition "firmly to insist on the exclusive right of the colonies to tax themselves." In late October, Jared Ingersoll sailed for England, arriving in early December with over 100 copies of the *Book of Reasons* (as it was also known) for distribution to influential Members of Parliament.

HUTCHINSON CRITIQUES

Massachusetts lieutenant governor Hutchinson interjected himself into the controversy by writing on November 9 to his friend Ebenezer Silliman.

> Your distinction between duties upon trade & internal taxes *agrees with the opinion of the people in England*, particularly your agent, & with the opinion of most people here. Mr. Bernard is full with you in it. I think it imprudent to oppose it, & therefore am silent, but it is for this reason only. I am for saving as much of our privileges as we can & *if the people of Eng. make this distinction*, I think it tends to strengthen us in our claim to exemption from internal taxes.
>
> Really there is no difference, & the fallacy of the argument lies here. It is your supposing duties upon trade to be *imposed for the sake of regulating trade*, whereas the professed design of the duties by the late Act [i.e., the Sugar Act] is to raise a revenue.

Hutchinson misreads the Connecticut position on this matter. The essay does not suppose the duties are "imposed for the sake of regulating trade." The essay is explicit about the propriety of imposing duties to raise revenue. Nonetheless, he next makes the point that duties on trade are equivalent to internal taxes.

To demonstrate there is no difference, and the danger of allowing that there is, he starts with the argument we saw in the introduction to part 2, that paying customs duty on a pipe of wine or an equivalently priced "duty of excise" on a per-gallon basis are equivalent: "the consumer pays just the same." But he goes further.

The rights of the people are alike affected in both cases. If they will stop where they are, I would not dispute their distinction with them, but if they intend to go on, there will be a necessity of doing it for *they may find duties on trade enough to drain us so thoroughly, that it will not be possible to pay internal taxes as a revenue to them or even to support government within ourselves.*[5]

This letter from Hutchinson demonstrates his complex (perhaps devious) thinking, coming so soon as it did after he coerced the Massachusetts assembly into agreeing to only a modest protest. The key is the phrase, "I think it imprudent to oppose it." (Hutchinson saw no distinction but thought there was political advantage in hiding opposition to external taxes.)

FITCH WEAKENS HIS STANCE

Fitch moved away from a denial of the authority of Parliament to impose internal taxes, fearing that an impolitic stance by the colonies might become, as he put it, "Detrimental to the Interest" of America. He wrote Richard Jackson on December 7.

You will doubtless before this comes to Hand have Received the Pamphlets by Mr. Ingersoll which Contain Reasons or Objections against Charging Stamp Duties or Internal Taxes on the Colonies.

In a single long, obsequious sentence, he disavows the objection to taxation.

We have avoided all Pretence of objection against the Authority or Power of the Parliament, as the Supreme Legislature of all the Kings Dominions, to Tax the Colonies, and have therefore Endeavoured only to Shew that the Exercise of Such Power, in that Particular Instance or in like Cases, will take away Part of our Antient Priviledges &c (which it is presumed the Parliament who are also Guardians of our Liberties will not do) and in the whole have Endeavoured to Express our Sentiments With becoming Modesty Decency & Submission and we trust as was intended without offence.

He also discusses an address (petition) to the House of Commons.

> The Colony have Desired me to prepare an Humble and Earnest
> address to the Parliament in Behalf and in the name of the Gov-
> ernor and Company of the Colony against an act being passed for
> Charging a Stamp Duty or an Internal Tax and transmit the same
> with the Reasons before mentioned to you in Order to be pre-
> ferred to the Parliament.

The petition, "being prepared in Consequence of the order of the
Assembly is herewith inclosed."[6] (In a later letter to Jackson he refers
to this as his "Address to the House of Commons praying against
being Charged with those Duties.")

RESULT OF THE PETITION TO THE HOUSE OF COMMONS

Jackson offered the Connecticut petition to the House of Commons
during debate on the Stamp Act on February 15, 1765. For the same
reasons we saw in the story told by agent Garth in chapter 7, the petition was rejected.

Connecticut makes a strong case against internal taxation. However,
duties for revenue are acceptable, even desirable if needed to defray
the "American Expence." That stance grants more power to Parliament than even the implicit acceptance of duties demonstrated by
Massachusetts.

On the other hand, except for the late squirming and waffling by
Fitch, Connecticut is clear that Parliament has no right to interfere
in the internal government and the (largely undefined) "essential
Rights, Immunities and Privileges."

In the papers by Bland and Fitch we see the beginning of a distinction between internal and external government, such a distinction
being used to put a limit on the authority of Parliament.

Nine

Rhode Island

I N CHAPTER 2 WE SAW *An Essay on the Trade of the Northern Colonies of Great Britain in North America,* written by Governor Stephen Hopkins. He published another influential essay in late 1764. It was one of three actions taken by Rhode Island: a call for intercolonial cooperation, a petition to the king, and the essay published as a pamphlet.

INITIAL LEGISLATIVE ACTION

The story starts with the final summer meeting of the General Assembly.[1]

> July 30, 1764
> It is voted and resolved, that His Honor the Governor [and others] are hereby, appointed a committee to confer and consult with any committee or committees that are, or shall be, appointed by any of the British colonies upon the continent of North America . . . to procure a repeal of the act of the sixth of His late Majesty, commonly called the sugar act [i.e., the act of 1733];

They seem to expect other colonies to still be concerned with the old Sugar Act. They are also concerned about the renewed Sugar Act and the planned stamp duty.

and also, of the act passed at the last session of Parliament, for levying several duties in the colonies, or in procuring the duties in the said last mentioned act, to be lessened; also, to prevent the levying a stamp duty upon the North American colonies, now under the consideration of Parliament; and, generally, for the prevention of all such taxes, duties or impositions, that may be proposed to be assessed upon the colonists, which may be inconsistent with their rights and privileges as British subjects.

The agent should also be involved.

And it is further voted and resolved, that His Honor the Governor, be, and he is hereby, requested to inform the agent of the steps this Assembly are taking; and to direct him, in the meantime, to do everything in his power, either alone, or by joining with the agents of the other governments, to effect the purposes intended by this Assembly.[2]

A CALL FOR UNITED ACTION

On October 8, the committee sent letters to the other colonies proposing that common viewpoints be gathered and suggesting they unite in a common defense of their liberties.

We have been appointed a committee by the General Assembly of the colony of Rhode Island to correspond, confer, and consult with any committee or committees that are or shall be appointed by any of the British colonies on the continent, and, *in concert with them, to prepare and form such representations* of the condition of the colonies, the rights of the inhabitants, and the interests of Great Britain, as connected with them, as may be most likely to be effectual to remove or alleviate the burdens which the colonists at present labor under and to prevent new ones being added.

The letter furthers the call for union implicit in the similar letter from Massachusetts.

The resolution of the House of Commons that they have a right
to tax the colonies, if carried into execution, will leave us nothing
to call our own. How far the united endeavours of all the colonies
might tend to prevent those evils, cannot be determined; but certainly it is worth their while to try every means in their power to
preserve every thing they have worth preserving.

The committee asks "whether your colony hath taken these matters under consideration; and if it hath, what methods have been
thought of, as most conducive to bring them to a happy issue."

If some method could be hit upon for collecting the sentiments of
each colony, and for uniting and *forming the substance of them
all into one common defence of the whole*; and this sent to England, and the several agents directed to join together in pushing
and pursuing it there, in the properest and most effectual manner,
it might be the most probable method to produce the end aimed
at.[3]

The idea of forming them into one common whole is at least a
hint of a meeting of the colonies.

PETITION AND ADDRESS TO THE KING

On October 30, the committee was given a further charge.

Prepare an address to His Majesty, for a redress of our grievances,
in respect to the duties, impositions, &c., already laid, and proposed to be laid, in this colony.[4]

The resulting *petition and address* is relatively concise. Here is the
entire document.

To the King's Most Excellent Majesty: the petition and address of
the Governor and Company of the English colony of Rhode Island
and Providence Plantations, in New England, in America; humbly
showeth:
    That this part of America was first planted by adventurers who
left England, their native country, by permission of Your Majesty's

royal predecessors; and, at their own expense, transported themselves to America, with great hardship and difficulty, settled among savages, and formed new colonies in the wilderness.

Before their departure, the terms they removed upon and the relation they should stand in to the mother country, in their emigrant state, were settled. They were to remain subject to the King and dependent on the kingdom of England; in return, they were to receive protection, and enjoy all the privileges of free born Englishmen.

All the above makes it clear that Rhode Island feels there is a contract with the king, a still-valid contract. In past years, there has been substantial adherence to the contract.

We acknowledge with great gratitude that the colonies have, at all times, received due succor, and the promised protection.

Our dependence hath been testified by a constant and ready obedience to all the commands of Your Majesty and your royal predecessors this, and the other colonies, having at all times, when called upon, raised men and money for the service of the crown and kingdom, with as much alacrity and in as large proportions as hath been done in Great Britain, the abilities of each considered.

With filial duty, we thankfully confess that from the first planting of these colonies, being more than one hundred and thirty years, we have fully enjoyed all the privileges and advantages that were promised to our ancestors, upon their first removal from England. Happy for us, and all the colonies, that we might still enjoy the blessings of the same mild and gracious government;

But the situation seems to have changed to such an extent that they must appeal to the king.

But here our fears intervene, and apprehensions of a different treatment from the mother country suffer us to go no further; we must be silent, or we must complain; we have a good cause; we have a gracious King.

We will, with the most submissive sentiments, open our grievances, and humbly lay our complaints before Your Majesty.

First complaint: high duty on foreign molasses (and its recent enforcement)—an economic grievance.

The restraints and burdens laid on the trade of these colonies by
a late act of Parliament are such, as if continued, must ruin it. The
commerce of this colony dependeth ultimately on foreign molasses, and *the duty on that being so much higher than it can possibly bear*, must prevent its importation; and by that means we
shall be deprived of our principal exports, totally lose our trade
to Africa, and *be rendered unable to make remittance to Great
Britain for the manufactures we cannot live without.*

They do not object to the fact of there being a molasses duty, simply to the high level. They sidestep the fact that the Sugar Act imposes
the duties at least partly for the purpose of revenue.
    Second complaint: courts of vice admiralty—a constitutional
grievance.

The extensive powers given by the same act to the courts of vice
admiralty in America, have a tendency, in a great measure, to *deprive the colonies of that darling privilege, trials by juries*, the un-
alienable birthright of every Englishman; and subjects the
inhabitants here to other great hardships and intolerable expenses;
as the seizer may take the goods of any person, though ever so
legally imported, and carry the trial into any distant province; and
if the judge can be prevailed upon to certify that there was probable cause of seizure, the claimer is without remedy; and herein
we are *unhappily distinguished from our fellow subjects in Britain.*

Third complaint: internal taxes—another constitutional grievance.

The colonies are much more alarmed on being informed that Your
Majesty's ministers have formed a resolution to establish *stamp
duties and other internal taxes to be collected within them.* This

design carried into execution, we humbly conceive, would tend to *deprive us of our just and long enjoyed rights*. We have hitherto possessed, as we thought, according to right, equal freedom with Your Majesty's subjects in Britain; *whose essential privilege it is to be governed only by laws to which themselves have some way consented, and not to be compelled to part with their property but as it is called for by authority of such laws.*

The taxation and the duties exacerbate the problem with lack of hard currency.

The great difficulty that has ever attended the trade of the colonies is a *scarcity of money*. This is occasioned by the very great balance against them in their trade with Britain. The further drawing large sums from them, by duties on importations of divers kinds of goods, by the post office, by stamp duties, and other internal taxes, will, in a short time, quite drain these colonies of the little money they have; totally *deprive them of the means of paying their debts* to, and continuing their trade with, Great Britain, and leave the people here poor and miserable.

The Americans have fulfilled their part of the contract and expect Britain to fulfill the royal promise.

Our ancestors, being loyal and dutiful subjects, removed and planted here under a royal promise, that, observing and fulfilling the conditions enjoined them, they and their children after them for ever, should hold and *enjoy equal rights, privileges and immunities with their fellow subjects in Britain*. The conditions have been faithfully kept by this colony.

Next is a good summary related to rights, trade, courts, and taxation.

We do therefore most humbly beseech Your Majesty that our freedom and all our just rights may be continued to us inviolate; That *our trade may be restored to its former condition*, and no

further limited, restrained and burdened, than becomes necessary
for the general good of *all Your Majesty's subjects*;
   That the courts of vice admiralty may not be vested with more
extensive powers in the colonies *than are given them by law in
Great Britain*;
   That the colonists may not be taxed but by the consent of their
own representatives, *as Your Majesty's other free subjects are.*

In closing, they aspire to retain advantages previously enjoyed.

That while Your Majesty's subjects justly exult in being governed
by the best of Kings, the father of his people, and guardian of their
liberties, your loyal colonies may not, in your glorious reign, *suffer
any diminution of the advantages they have hitherto enjoyed.*
Whatever may be determined concerning them, the Governor and
Company of Rhode Island will ever unalterably remain—
Your Majesty's most loyal, most dutiful and most obedient sub-
jects.
Stephen Hopkins
November 29, 1764

   This is really a pretty mild protest: maintain our rights, restore
our trade, sensibly limit the power of the courts, and don't tax us.
Invoking "the consent of their own representatives" indirectly denies
the taxing authority of Parliament but avoids such a direct statement.
A point not to be overlooked is that the appeal is not to Parliament
to change its direction but for the king to intercede with Parliament.
The address was sent to agent Joseph Sherwood.

STEPHEN HOPKINS: THE RIGHTS OF COLONIES EXAMINED
In parallel with the address to the king, the governor prepared a
longer statement of the position of the colony: *The Rights of Colonies
Examined.* It was approved by the General Assembly on November
30, first printed in the *Records of the Colony of Rhode Island,* and
later published by direction of the assembly in the *Providence
Gazette* on December 22. It was reprinted by other colonial newspapers and issued as a pamphlet, including in a London edition.

Hopkins's principal assertion—the central right of the colonies—is that Americans cannot be taxed by Parliament. Along the way, he points out the adverse economic effect of the Sugar Act. Although he finds no constitutional objection to the molasses duty, he criticizes it as unjust as applied to Rhode Island. He starts with a statement of his method of proceeding. The first sentence is gripping.

> *Liberty is the greatest blessing that men enjoy, and slavery the heaviest curse that human nature is capable of.* [We must balance liberty and law, so] we will consider the British constitution as it at present stands . . . and from thence endeavor to find the measure of the magistrate's power and the people's obedience.
>
> This glorious constitution, the best that ever existed among men, will be confessed by all to be founded by compact and established by consent of the people. By this most beneficent compact *British subjects are to be governed only agreeable to laws to which themselves have some way consented,* and are not to be compelled to part with their property but as it is called for by the authority of such laws.

A strong statement, but we will see later that he dances away from the need for consent when dealing with the imposition of duties.

> On the contrary, those who are governed at the will of another, or of others, and whose property may be taken from them by taxes or otherwise without their own consent and against their will, *are in the miserable condition of slaves.*

He quotes a well-known political philosopher.

> "For liberty solely consists in an independency upon the will of another; and by the name of slave we understand a man who can neither dispose of his person or goods, but enjoys all at the will of his master," says Sidney on government.

He refers to the still-valid Rhode Island charter that promises that those who established the colony "and their successors forever

should be free, should be partakers and sharers in all the privileges
and advantages of the then English, now British constitution."

> Colonies that came out *from a kingdom renowned for liberty,*
> *from a constitution founded on compact,* from a people of all the
> sons of men the most tenacious of freedom; . . . that removed on
> a *firm reliance of a solemn compact and royal promise and grant*
> *that they and their successors forever should be free,* should be
> partakers and sharers in all the privileges and advantages of the
> then English, now British constitution.

Compact is not the only source of rights. Although they are promised and granted, rights in fact are inherent, not privileges, not in-
dulgences, not favors that might be withdrawn. This is part of the
central meaning of the essay, the reason why they cannot be taxed
by Parliament.

> British subjects in America have equal rights with those in Britain;
> *they do not hold those rights as a privilege granted them,* nor
> enjoy them as a grace and favor bestowed, but possess them as an
> inherent, indefeasible right, as they and their ancestors were free-
> born subjects, justly and naturally entitled to all the rights and ad-
> vantages of the British constitution.

He buttresses the inherent right by introducing long usage, pointing out that heretofore "the British legislative and executive powers
have considered the colonies as possessed of these rights."

Both sides have, thus far, fulfilled the contract; but recently, not
so much. He lays the blame first of all on the ministry (a common
allegation of American protests), then on the actions of Parliament.

> But here the scene seems to be unhappily changing: the British
> ministry, whether induced by a jealousy of the colonies, by false
> informations, or by some alteration in the system of political gov-
> ernment, we have no information.

He briefly deals with the adverse effect of the changed scene: admiralty courts, interference with trade of the colonies, and "a reso-

lution that it might be necessary to establish *stamp duties* and other internal taxes to be collected within them. This act and this resolution have caused great uneasiness and consternation among the British subjects on the continent of America."

He embarks on a wide-ranging discussion about the relative roles of Parliament and the colonial legislatures, starting with a definition of a broad area of authority for Parliament. (But by defining its powers, he effectively places limits on Parliament.) His thinking is not as elaborate as that of Richard Bland, but he is also on the road to distinguishing and defining the roles of internal and external spheres of government.

> In the first place, let it be considered that although each of the colonies hath a legislature within itself to take care of its interests and provide for its peace and internal government, yet there are many *things of a more general nature*, quite out of the reach of these particular legislatures, which it is necessary should be regulated, ordered, and governed.

So internal government is "take care of its interests and provide for its peace." He elaborates on "more general nature."

> One of this kind is the commerce of the whole British empire, taken collectively, and that of each kingdom and colony in it as it makes a part of that whole. Indeed, everything that concerns the proper interest and fit government of the whole commonwealth, of keeping the peace, and subordination of all the parts towards the whole and one among another, must be considered in this light.

He does not use the phrase *external government* but "commerce of the whole British empire," and similar phrases are certainly external government.

> These, with all other matters of a general nature, it is *absolutely necessary should have a general power* to direct them, some supreme and overruling authority with power to make laws and form regulations *for the good of all*, and to compel their execution

and observation. [The] parliament of Great Britain, that grand and august legislative body, must, from the nature of their authority and the necessity of the thing, be justly vested with this power.

He is using the word *power* in the sense of rightful authority.

Hence it becomes the indispensable duty of every good and loyal subject cheerfully to obey and patiently submit to all the acts, laws, orders, and regulations that may be made and passed by Parliament for directing and governing all these *general matters*.

A crucial phrase: "general matters." He means, in fact, *only* general matters, thereby further stressing limitation of the power of Parliament.

He changes focus to the immediate issues of 1764, arguing that the Americans were inadequately consulted about the Sugar Act; otherwise, "no reasonable man can suppose it ever would have passed at all, in the manner it now stands." The objection to the threepence duty is economic.

A duty of three pence per gallon on foreign molasses is well known to every man in the least acquainted with it to be much *higher than that article can possibly bear*, and therefore must operate as an absolute prohibition.

He repeats some of the arguments we saw in his earlier essay (January), then raises a new issue: justice.

The charging foreign molasses with this high duty will not affect all the colonies equally, nor any other near so much as this of Rhode Island, whose trade depended much more on foreign molasses and on distilleries than that of any others; *this must show that raising money for the general service of the crown or of the colonies by such a duty will be extremely unequal and therefore unjust.*

He is unclear here about an "unjust" duty. There is a certain tension in his reasoning, since he later is adamant that Parliament can impose duties "at pleasure." He finishes the line of reasoning about duties by asserting that whether the duty stops the molasses trade or "all their money is taken from them by paying the duty," both America and Great Britain are losers. But the quibble about the high duty pales before his next attack on the effect of the threat of stamp duties.

> The resolution of the House of Commons, come into during the same session of Parliament, asserting their rights to establish stamp duties and internal taxes to be collected in the colonies without their own consent, hath much more, and for much more reason, *alarmed the British subjects in America than anything that had ever been done before.* These resolutions, carried into execution, the colonies cannot help but consider as a manifest violation of their just and long enjoyed rights. For it must be confessed by all men that they who are taxed at pleasure by others cannot possibly have any property, can have nothing to be called their own. They who have no property can have no freedom, but are indeed reduced to the most abject slavery.

He does not use the word *unconstitutional*, but there can be no doubt of his meaning.

Next we see a practical matter: elected officials will, of course, choose (even find it necessary) to take off taxes from their constituents if they can lay them somewhere else.

> And indeed, if the people in America are to be taxed by the representatives of the people in Britain, their malady is an increasing evil that must always grow greater by time.
>
> *Whatever burdens are laid upon the Americans will be so much taken off the Britons; and the doing this will soon be extremely popular,* and those who put up to be members of the House of Commons must obtain the votes of the people by promising to take more and more of the taxes off them by putting it on the Americans. This must most assuredly be the case, and it will not be in the power even of the Parliament to prevent it; the people's private interest will be concerned and will govern them; they will

have such, and only such, representatives as will act agreeable to this their interest.

As a consequence, "The subjects in the colonies will be taxed at the will and pleasure of their fellow subjects in Britain."

He moves to a broader issue: the British Empire is not a single state but separate governments, which Hopkins calls an *imperial state*.

In an imperial state, which consists of *many separate governments* each of which hath peculiar privileges, and of which kind it is evident the empire of Great Britain is, no single part, though greater than another part, is by that superiority entitled to make laws for or to tax such lesser part; but *all laws and all taxations which bind the whole must be made by the whole.*

This is an astounding statement for 1764—that each colony is a separate government. It is essentially a forerunner of Bland's view (expressed later, in 1766) that each separate government is a "distinct State, independent as to their internal Government."

But their autonomous nature is always in the context of his earlier qualification that for "matters of a general nature it is absolutely necessary" that there be a general power—Parliament—to make laws for the good of all.

The Parliament, it is confessed, have power to regulate the trade of the whole empire; and hath it not full power, by this means, to *draw all the money and all the wealth of the colonies into the mother country at pleasure?*

He has more to say, and says it, but finally comes to:

May the same divine goodness . . . perpetuate the sovereignty of the British constitution, and the filial dependency and happiness of all the colonies.
Providence, in New England, November 30, 1764.[6]

In that he acknowledges the authority to levy duties "at pleasure," his attitude about external taxes is similar to the authority granted by Governor Fitch of Connecticut that Parliament may levy duties "as the supreme Power may judge proper." Although taxation binding the whole must be agreed to by all, the same restriction does not apply to duties.

Let's look at the contrast between taxes and duties; he had earlier denied the right of Parliament to *tax* at pleasure, while he admits the rightful authority to "draw all the money" through trade regulation. This juxtaposition of disallowed taxation with the right of Parliament to impose duties at pleasure makes it clear that his rights-based objection is restricted to internal taxes, the stamp duties.

RESULT OF THE PETITION AND THE PAMPHLET

Sherwood wrote on April 11, 1765, to report the disposition of the Rhode Island address to the king and the Hopkins essay. The news was not good.

> The Papers and Letters and also the Address to the King has been delivered to the Secretary of State, that being the usual and proper Channel; I do not apprehend any Benefit can arise from Addressing the King on Affairs of Trade and Commerce. These Affairs are left to the Board of Trade and Parliament.

The petition was thereafter ignored. Nor was the pamphlet useful, the act having been passed before it arrived.

> No Benefit could possibly arise from Reprinting it here; many Pamphlets have been Published here on the Occasion. I shall pay due regard to the Intimation respecting Extracting the Quintessence of the whole and Printing for the use of the Members, but that must be a Consideration for the next Year as it is too late to carry into Execution a scheme of this sort this Session.[7]

Rhode Island protested the impending stamp duties as unconstitutional. The stricture against Parliament making law that went beyond "matters of a general nature" was similar to Richard Bland's limitation on Parliament expressed as restricted to external government. The protest against the levy of duties for revenue was more nuanced, objecting to the economic burden but making no constitutional protest, even acknowledging that Parliament could lay duties "at pleasure."

Ten

Other American Colonies

F OUR ADDITIONAL COLONIES LODGED PROTESTS IN 1764: Pennsylvania, New Jersey, North Carolina, and South Carolina.

PENNSYLVANIA

As a consequence of an internal political controversy, Pennsylvania lodged no direct protest with the king or Parliament. The colony stated its grievance in the form of instructions to its agent, Richard Jackson.

Along the way, Benjamin Franklin carried on a spirited dialogue with friends. Franklin was continually the optimist about trade and taxation issues, believing that Great Britain would take no action to harm the colonies. First of all, he believed in the good will of the ministry. Second, he believed that Britain was already gaining from America as much as was possible. In April he wrote a friend, "What you get from us in Taxes you must lose in Trade. The Cat can yield but her Skin. And as you must have the whole Hide, if you first cut Thongs out of it, 'tis at your own Expence."

Franklin wrote Jackson on June 1. "We see in the Papers that an Act is pass'd for granting certain Duties on Goods in the British Colonies, &c. but are not yet acquainted with its Contents." While the contents were unknown, the enforcement actions of the Royal

Navy were clear enough. Franklin makes this observation, taking a different view than most Americans.

> The Men of War station'd in our several Ports are very active in their new Employment of Custom house Officers; a Portmanteau cannot go between here and New York without being search'd. Every Boat stopt and examin'd, and much Incumbrance by that means brought upon all Business. Undoubtedly the illicit Trade ought to be stopt; and if all this Strictness is necessary to that end, I have the less Objection to it.[1]

As the newly elected speaker of the assembly, Franklin sent Jackson these instructions on September 22; they are forceful, approaching a denial of the authority of Parliament to tax the colonies, certainly raising the constitutional question. (Some of the text below parrots or imitates wording in the letter of June 25 from Massachusetts.)

> The Representatives of the Freemen of the Province of Pennsylvania, in General Assembly met, having received Information of the Resolutions of the House of Commons respecting the Stamp Duties, and other Taxes, proposed to be laid on the British Colonies, do humbly conceive that the measures proposed as aforesaid, if carried into execution, will have a tendency to deprive the good people of this Province of their *most essential rights as British Subjects*, and of the rights granted to them by the Royal Charter.

Further, the rights are "confirmed by Laws of this Province, which have received the Royal Approbation." Based on the rights, the assembly claims for Pennsylvania the exclusive right to levy taxes.

> That by the said Charter, among other privileges, the right of assessing their own taxes, and of being free from any impositions but those that are made by their own representatives, is fully granted to the people of this Province. And besides, we apprehend that this is the indubitable right of all the colonists as Englishmen.
> That said, charter and laws are certainly of the same validity, with respect to the rights therein granted to the people here, as

the laws and statutes of England with regard to the privileges derived under them to the people of England, and that it appears to us as great injustice to divest the people of this province of the privileges held under the former, as to disfranchise the people of England of those rights they claim under Magna Carta itself, or any other laws of Great Britain.

The assembly is explicit about heading off the planned stamp duties.

These, with other Reasons, and *in particular the Information we have received,* that the Ministry are desirous of consulting the Ease, Interest and good Will of the Colonies, prevail on us to hope, that an humble and dutiful Remonstrance to the Parliament, pointing out the Inconsistency of those Measures with the Rights and Privileges thus purchased, and solemnly granted and confirmed to the People of this Colony, may have its Use in prevailing on the Parliament to lay aside their Intention of imposing Stamp Duties, or *laying any other Impositions or Taxes* whatsoever on the Colonies, which may be destructive of their respective Rights.

Specific instructions.

The House of Assembly therefore most earnestly request you will exert your utmost Endeavours with the Ministry and Parliament to prevent any such Impositions and Taxes, or any other impositions or Taxes on the Colonists from being laid by the Parliament, inasmuch as they neither are or can be represented, under their present Circumstances, in that Legislature.

Nor can the Parliament, at the great Distance they are from the Colonies, be properly informed, so as to enable them to lay such Taxes and Impositions with Justice and Equity, the Circumstances of the Colonies being all different one from the other.

This we request you will do, either by an humble Address to the British Parliament, or in any other Manner, which to you shall appear to promise the most Success.

Also do something about that aggravating Sugar Act.

You will also be pleased to exert your Endeavours to obtain a Repeal, or at least an Amendment, of the Act for regulating the Sugar Trade, which we apprehend must prove extremely detrimental to the Trade of the Continental Colonies in America.

The letter ends with a modest instruction about cooperation with the other agents.

Upon the Whole, they submit these Affairs entirely to your Management and Discretion, and doubt not but you will conduct every Matter for the Interest of the Colonies in the best Manner possible, wherein *perhaps it may not be amiss to unite with the Agents of the other Provinces.*
Signed by Order of the House, Benjamin Franklin, Speaker.[2]

NEW JERSEY

The New Jersey response also was limited to instructions to its agent, Joseph Sherwood.

On August 24, the speaker of the New Jersey General Assembly, Robert Ogden, sent to Attorney General Courtland Skinner a copy of the June 25 letter from Massachusetts.

The enclosed is a copy of what I Recd from . . . the Colony of the Massachusetts Bay, which I now send for your Perusal & advice; the affair is Serious & Greatly Concerns all the Colonies to unite & exert themselves to the utmost to Keep off the Threatening blow of Imposing Taxes Duties &c. so Destructive to the Libertys the Colonies hitherto enjoyed. . . . If you think it of Importance Beg you would . . . write to His Excellency [the Governor] & Desire him to Give us a Meeting as Early in September as Possible.[3]

Although the governor did not call the assembly into session, the committee of correspondence wrote agent Sherwood on September 10.

If anything comes on the Stage next Session of Parliament either for repealing the Duties laid on the Trade of the Northern Colonies and prohibiting a paper Currency at last Session, or for adding any thing new by way of Tax on this Colony, the Committee of Correspondents direct that you will humbly & Dutifully Set forth In the name and on Behalf of this Colony that we look upon all Taxes laid upon us without our Consent as a fundamental infringement of the Rights and privileges Secured to us as English Subjects and by Charter.

New Jersey, although a royal colony, held an attitude much like Virginia, that its charter privileges (in this case from back when it was a proprietary colony) still had validity.

The more active and expensive part of the Opposition we expect will lie upon the other Colonies who are abundantly more Concerned in Trade, yet it is Necessary so far to cooperate with them as to Show the Colonies are unanimously of One Mind.[4]

NORTH CAROLINA

The North Carolina protest was made only to the governor, but it was aggressive in tone and shared with New York the distinction of recognizing the Sugar Act duties as taxes. On October 31, the assembly made this protest.

To his Excellency Arthur Dobbs, Esquire, Captain General, Governor and Commander-in-Chief in and over his Majesty's Province of North Carolina.

We his Majesty's most dutiful subjects, the Members of the Assembly of North Carolina return your Excellency our thanks for your Speech at the opening of this Session.

First, the economic grievance.

As the *Tax on Trade* [Sugar Act duties], lately imposed by Act of Parliament on the British Colonies in America must tend greatly to the Hindrance of Commerce and be severely felt by the Industrious Inhabitants of this Province. . . . [and so on].

Then the constitutional objection, still referring to the "Tax on Trade."

It is with the utmost concern we observe our Commerce Circumscribed in its most beneficial Branches, diverted from its natural Channel, and Burthened with new Taxes and Impositions laid on us without our Privity and Consent, and against what we esteem our *Inherent right and Exclusive privilege of Imposing our own Taxes.*
JOHN ASHE Speaker.[5]

SOUTH CAROLINA

South Carolina offered no official legislative protest to Great Britain. However, based on extensive guidance from the committee of correspondence, agent Charles Garth prepared a petition to the House of Commons.

Protest and Petition

On September 4, the committee of correspondence wrote Garth to make it clear that South Carolina is in opposition to the impending taxes.

We have particularly in charge from the House, to direct you to make all opposition you possibly can, in conjunction with the agent[s] of the other colonies, in the laying a *stamp duty, or any other tax* by act of Parliament on the colonies.

Here is the constitutional argument.

The first, and in our opinion the principal reason, against such a measure, is its inconsistency with that inherent right of every British subject, *not to be taxed but by his own consent, or that of his representative.*

(This point made by South Carolina combines nicely with the phrase above from North Carolina: "laid on us without our Privity and Consent, and against what we esteem our *Inherent right and Exclusive privilege of Imposing our own Taxes.*" It is not too much to say, "Here, in essence, before the debate had really begun was the whole American case against taxation by Parliament.")[6]

Although South Carolina will "submit most dutifully at all times to acts of Parliament," the colonists expect equal treatment with other British subjects.

> Yet we think it incumbent on us humbly to remonstrate against such as appear oppressive, hoping that when that august body come to consider this matter they will view it in a most favorable light, and not deprive us of our birthright, and thereby reduce us to the condition of vassals and tributaries. This privilege is due to us as British subjects, *born under the same allegiance and form of government, and entitled to the inestimable rights of the same laws and customs,* founded on the reason and common sense of mankind.

Only the direct representatives of the people can know what taxes to levy.

> For doubtless the representatives of the people of any province must best know in what manner supplies may be most conveniently raised by their respective constituents; and, by residing in this province, we are sure we become not less but more useful and beneficial to our mother country, where we do actually contribute all in our power to relieve her from the great load of debt she lies under.

The impending stamp duties place

> additional and unexpected impositions on a people already over-burthened with taxes and deeply in debt, who have so sickly a climate and such inclement seasons to struggle withal, as necessarily expose them to a much more expensive way of living than they would be liable to in a more healthy and temperate country.[7]

Garth responded on December 26.

The directions for opposition in conjunction with the agents for the other Colonies to the laying a Stamp Duty or any other tax by Act of Parliament on the Colonies I shall most duly observe.

He is organizing opposition.

At present the agents are not all in town; I have wrote and spoke to several of them already in order to learn what instructions they have been furnished with for the regulation of their conduct in the ensuing Sessions. I intend soon to propose a general meeting in order to consider of the proper steps to be taken in case the intended Stamp Bill should be brought into Parliament, for my opinion is as the Colonies oppose, they ought to oppose upon a point of this importance in such manner as most to command the attention of the Legislature.

Garth prepared a petition himself to the House of Commons.

It will be unnecessary to make particular observations upon the arguments you have furnished me; I think them so full and particular that whenever call'd for I shall have sufficient matter from whence to frame my petition.

He offers a good argument for why petitions should be accepted.

Tho' the House seem'd last year to express themselves so strongly upon the power of Parliament, I conceive the Colonies have a right to dispute (unrepresented as they are) and may, the exertion of a power like this which is thought of, without disputing the general superintending power of Parliament over every part of the Dominions subject to the Crown of Great Britain in cases where for the good of the whole its execution should be made necessary, but this cannot be said to be that case.[8]

When we looked at the result of the Virginia petition, I related Garth's story told in a letter of February 17, 1765. In the same letter, he discussed the South Carolina petition, hoping that the mild address he drew up himself would fare better.

> I was in hopes to have had it received; not I confess, from any flattering apprehension that it could have prevented the Stamp Bill taking place . . . but if it could have been admitted, a precedent would have been established that would have prevented any future attempts to tax America, until at least the public in America had been appriz'd thereof.

He did try to introduce his petition.

> Notwithstanding the fate of the Virginia petition, I determin'd to offer mine on the part of S. Carolina, and accordingly mov'd to bring it up; I was call'd upon to state the contents, which done, *the House were of opinion it tended to question the right of Parliament to exercise this power of taxation*, and being likewise against a Money Bill, was also refus'd.[9]

EPILOGUE

B ritish leaders heard a single message in the protests of 1764: Americans deny the right of Parliament to levy taxes on the colonies. In doing so, they deny the supremacy of Parliament and deny "the very sovereignty of this kingdom." In response, Parliament levied stamp duties, establishing the very taxes protested by the Americans.

AMERICAN PROTESTS ARRIVE

News about American concerns, unofficial but accurate, reached Great Britain in early December. This appeared in the *London Chronicle* on December 6, 1764.

> Boston (New England, Oct. 5)
> The late act of parliament (possibly for want of a thorough un-derstanding) gives some uneasiness to the people of this province, and it is said of the northern colonies in general; and the fears of being taxed internally, by the parliament, while we have no rep-resentation on the spot, are alarming to men of the greatest pen-etration and judgement among us.

The writer reports that Parliament will soon meet and will be ad-dressing "the defiance of the colonies from Great Britain."[1]

FIRST BRITISH REACTION

The *Journal* of the Board of Trade for December 11, 1764, shows its reaction to Bernard's letter of June 29 and Colden's letter of September 20.

> Their lordships took into consideration the printed votes of the House of Representatives of the Province of Massachusetts Bay in their last Session of Assembly transmitted to the Board by Governor Bernard, as also a book therein referred to, and an address of the Assembly of New York to the Lieutenant Governor, and his answer thereto; and it appearing to their lordships, that in the said votes and address, *the Acts and resolutions of the British Parliament were treated with indecent disrespect, and principles of a dangerous nature and tendency adopted and avowed*, it was agreed to lay the said papers before his Majesty in Council, and a representation to his Majesty thereupon was prepared, agreed to and signed.[2]

The representation went to the king that day, starting with censure of Massachusetts.

> May it please Your Majesty,
>   Francis Bernard Esq., your Majestys Governor of the Province of Massachusetts Bay, having transmitted to us the printed Votes of the House of Representatives of that Province in their last Session of Assembly, containing amongst other things their Resolutions and proceedings upon several letters received from their Agent in Great Britain & also containing a letter to the said Agent from a Committee of the House of Representatives, which, contrary to the usual practice, was without the concurrence of the Governor and Council appointed to instruct him; in which letter the Acts and Resolutions of the Legislature of Great Britain are, we humbly conceive, treated with the most indecent disrespect, principles of the most dangerous nature and tendency openly avowed, and the Assemblies of other Colonies invited in most extraordinary manner to adopt the same opinions. We think it our duty humbly to lay these Votes before your Majesty, together with

a book referred to therein, printed & published at Boston and since reprinted and published in London.

(The Board of Trade had not yet received the Massachusetts official petition of November 3, but even later, not mollified by the modest statement, British perceptions were influenced by the outrageous actions of the assembly.)

The board condemns the address of September 11 from the New York Assembly.

We likewise crave leave humbly to lay before your Majesty the Copy of an Address of the Assembly of New York to the Lieutenant Governor of that Province, and of his prudent and becoming answer thereto; in which address the said Assembly avow opinions and make declarations of the same dangerous tendency with those of the Assembly of the Massachusetts Bay.

And it concludes that these matters are simply over the head of the board.

These proceedings which are in our judgment calculated to raise groundless suspicion & distrust in the minds of your Majesty's good subjects in the Colonies, and have the strongest tendency to subvert those principles of constitutional relation & dependance upon which the Colonies were originally established, contain certain matter of so high importance that we shall not presume to offer any opinion what may be proper to be done thereupon; submitting it to your Majesty to pursue such measures as your Majesty shall in your great wisdom and with the advice of your Council think most prudent and necessary.[3]

On December 19, the Privy Council evaluated the representation from the Board of Trade and offered its opinion to the king. "That it is a matter of the highest consequence to the Kingdom, and the Legislature of Great Britain, and worthy the Consideration of Parliament."[4]

REAFFIRMING THE RIGHT OF TAXING THE COLONIES

The initial American protests gave Grenville pause. He chose to seek confirmation of his constitutional position of the right of Parliament to levy inland duties. Of greatest importance is his discussion with Lord Chief Justice Mansfield, the most eminent jurist of the day. On December 24 he received support for his position. "The question certainly does not want this, or any other authority, yet it will be a striking alteration to ignorant people."[5]

Grenville also consulted with Charles Jenkinson, who provided a memorandum asserting in no uncertain terms the authority of Parliament.

> The Right of Taxing the Colonies not merely an Act of Power but a Constitutional Act of Legislation founded upon Principle and justified by Precedent.
>
> The principle is that all who are entitled to Protection ought equally to bear the Burthen of It, and that They who have the Management of that Protection can be the only Judges of what that Burthen should be.[6]

PURPOSE OF THE STAMP ACT: RIGHT, NOT REVENUE

British leaders, outraged at the nature of American protests, developed new motivation for the stamp duties. More important than revenue was demonstration of the right to levy taxes on the colonies. Let's look at the change in rationale.

When Thomas Whately wrote John Temple on November 5, 1764, his concern was with revenue.

> Burthen'd as this country is with debt and with expence, some attention must be had to revenue, and the Colonies must contribute their share; tho' I believe, as there is no idea of charging them very highly, the part they will bear will be found much less than their proportion.[7]

However, only three months later, as Whately expressed it to Temple on February 9, 1765, the concern was no longer with revenue but with establishing the right to levy the tax.

The *great measure of the sessions* is the American Stamp Act. I give it the appellation of a great measure on account of the important point it establishes *the right of Parliament to lay an internal tax upon the Colonies.* We wonder here that it ever was doubted. There is not a single member of Parliament to be found that will dispute it, & the proposition of a stamp duty seem'd so reasonable when made last week to the House, that [it was easily passed] & the expediency only was debated. This puts an end to all opposition to the principle of the bill, & now the rates are the only question.[8]

As more American refusals to recognize the authority of Parliament came to light, the need to establish the right to levy the tax became ever more important. The reaction of British leaders is shown by this blunt letter of February 14 from a knowledgeable undersecretary of state to a colleague.

What you have heard of the Refractoriness of the Colonies is very true. There are several Resolutions of American Assemblies, in which they almost deny or strongly remonstrate against the Right of the Parliament to tax them, which are directed by Order in Council to be laid before the Parliament. *But first it is thought proper to establish that Right by a new execution of it, and in the strongest instance, an internal Tax, that of the Stamp Duty.* It is remarkable that the Colonies can find no Champions to oppose that Measure and that there are Petitions in town from some of them to the two Houses which they can not get any Member to present.[9]

THE PETITIONS

Only three petitions were offered to the House of Commons: those of Virginia, Connecticut, and South Carolina. Whether to accept any petition at all was a topic of debate on February 15, 1765. "Grenville at once quoted the precedent of 8 March 1733, and later denied the opposition claim that the year's delay of the stamp duties had been intended to give the colonies time to petition. Procedural expert Jeremiah Dyson admitted the rule to reject such petitions was 'not antient,' but urged that 'practice made the rule, and tis dangerous to break it.'"[10] The point was argued back and forth, but ultimately the petitions were rejected based both on the precedent and the tone of the petitions. Whately wrote Temple a few months later with an explanation. "To receive the petitions would have been an acknowledgment that ye right was questionable, which we cannot admit."[11]

THE STORY OF 1765

The story of 1765 is that Parliament passes the Stamp Act. The Americans protest, not only with resolves, petitions, and essays but with an organized boycott of British products by nonimportation associations and with violent resistance that prevents the Stamp Act from going into effect.

Massachusetts governor Bernard on November 23, 1765, wrote his friend and sounding board Secretary at War Lord Barrington. Bernard reflected on the situation in late 1764, at which time he had thought "that the Regulation & Reformation of the American Governments was then become a necessary Work." But he did not endorse the resulting taxation of 1765. "A little Consideration would have made it at least doubtfull whether an inland Taxation of the Americans was practicable or equitable at that Time."

> It must have been supposed that such an Innovation as a Parliamentary Taxation would cause a great Alarm & meet with much Opposition in most parts of America; It was quite new to the people & had no visible Bounds set to it.

The American objections foreshadowed the later violent reaction.

> The Americans declared that they would not submit to it *before the Act passed*; & there was the greatest probability that it would require the utmost Power of Government to carry it into Execution.

Bernard makes a wistful wish to return to a more peaceful time, before the British policy change that became evident in 1764.

It were much to be wished that America could be brought to the State it was in two Years ago, when there was a general Disposition to submit to regulations & requisitions necessary to the Reformation of the Governments & ascertaining their relation to Great Britain. But that Time is past & not to be retrieved.

The Americans "seem to be resolved that their Idea of their Relation to Great Britain . . . shall be the standard of it."

The Question will not be whether there shall be a Stamp Act or not; but whether America *shall or shall not be Subject to the Legislature of Great Britain.*[12]

THE CONTINUING STORY

The story of 1766 is that Parliament repeals the Stamp Act but enacts legislation declaring the right to legislate for America "in all cases whatsoever." A modification to the Sugar Act reduces the molasses duty to one penny per gallon while at the same time transforming the duty into a true tax by making it applicable to all imported molasses (including that from British sugar colonies). The Americans, joyous over repeal of the stamp duties and happy with the reduction of the molasses duty to one penny, acquiesce; they make no protest to the duties of the Sugar Act. Further, "despite the fact that the act of 1766 was as clearly a revenue measure as any other law of the times, almost no attention seems to have been paid to it on either side of the water."[13]

The story of 1767 is the imposition of new taxes. The lack of protest about port duties being used for the collection of taxes reinforces the British understanding that Americans accept external taxation. On May 13, Charles Townshend, the chancellor of the exchequer, declared in the House of Commons that although he was "clear in opinion that this country had a power of taxation of every sort, and in every case," he planned

to lay taxes upon America, but not internal taxes, because though he did not acknowledge the distinction, it was accepted by many Americans and this was sufficient.[14]

On May 16, the London agent of Connecticut wrote home to report Townshend's comments of May 13.

> Although he did not in the least doubt the right of Parliament to
> tax the Colonies internally, and that he knew no difference be-
> tween internal and external taxes . . . yet since the Americans were
> pleased to make that distinction he was willing to indulge them,
> and chose for that reason to *confine himself to regulations of
> trade, by which a sufficient revenue might be raised in America.*[15]

The resulting Townshend Revenue Act (formally, "An Act for
granting certain duties in the British colonies and plantations in
America") had barely a nod toward trade regulation; it levied taxes
on products imported from Great Britain—collected as port duties.

The story of 1768 and 1769 is that—to British surprise—the
Americans view those Townshend duties as unconstitutional taxes
and protest with petitions, nonimportation, violence. Parliamentary
strategist William Dowdeswell, in a long political and philosophical
letter of 1768, observes that the duties are not "grievous burdens on
the colonies," then brings out the true grievance and the necessary
British response.

> The people there [make their stand] against the general principle
> of raising any revenue in America.

But for Parliament to repeal the act "would be avoiding the real
question."

> A repeated opposition . . . upon a principle directed against all duties
> for revenue must be met. It must either be admitted which is timidity,
> weakness, irresolution & inconsistency; or it must be resisted & ye
> arms of this Country must be exerted against her colonies.

He points out a real inconsistency in the American protests.

> If the Americans found their petition upon that principle of right
> which goes against raising any revenue at all in America, they

ought to pray not only [against the Townshend duties] but against
all duties laid for revenue, [including] *those very duties which a
few years ago we were told they were so willing to pay.*

He even anticipates that the Americans would "therefore extend
their opposition even to a reduced duty on the molasses." He concludes that "the distinction between external & internal taxes has
been found frivolous."[16]

In Parliament in 1769, in the midst of the controversy over the
duties, Townshend's original rationale was criticized; it was defended
with this assertion.

He was anxious to impose taxes that would be acceptable to the
Americans; but in these hopes *he was misled by the Americans
themselves*; who said to him, "take the tax; let it but bear the appearance of port duties, and it will not be objected to."[17]

Such a statement is a manifestation of the disconnect between
British and American thinking. Before 1767 (and we saw this going
on in 1764), Americans rejected taxes but not customs duties *for the
regulation of trade.* The British saw that position as being acceptance
of taxes as long as they were levied as customs duties, collected at
the ports. Looking back, we can view the misunderstanding in either
of two ways: the British were misled or the Americans were misun-
derstood.

Finally, it was in 1768 and 1769 that the Americans did begin to
reassess their acceptance of the Sugar Act duties. In January 1768,
Governor Bernard explained the new American perception. "The difference between an external and an internal tax is that the former is
imposed for the regulation of trade & the latter for raising a Revenue." And, as a result, "All the Port Duties imposed upon America
are internal Taxes."[18] The Americans simply dropped the distinction
of previous years. Seeing that external taxation "was as much designed to collect revenue as the 'internal' Stamp Act, the distinction,
never surely grasped, at once dissolved."[19]

Edmund Burke in 1774 put it this way to the House of Commons.

You revived the scheme of taxation [referring to the Townshend Revenue Act], and thereby filled the minds of the colonists with new jealousy, and all sorts of apprehensions; *then it was that they quarrelled with the old taxes,* as well as the new: then it was, *and not till then,* that they questioned all the parts of your legislative power; and by the battery of such questions have shaken the solid structure of this empire to its deepest foundations.[20]

THE END OF THE STORY

By 1774, both the Americans and the British understood the importance of the events of a decade earlier. First, let's listen again to Edmund Burke. He stresses that 1764 and the Sugar Act marked a turning point in the relationship between America and Great Britain. "No act avowedly for the purpose of revenue," he says, "is found in the statute book until . . . 1764." It was the Sugar Act that "opened a new principle." The Sugar Act established the new policy of taxing the colonies. "A complete American Revenue Act was made in all the forms, and with a full avowal of the right, equity, policy, and even necessity of taxing the Colonies, without any formal consent of theirs."[21]

The Americans, in the First Continental Congress on October 14, 1774, made a set of declarations and resolves:

Whereas, since the close of the last war, the British parliament, claiming a power of right to bind the people of America by statutes in all cases whatsoever, hath, in some acts, expressly imposed taxes on them . . .

A long preamble was followed by resolves, including calling out the Sugar Act of 1764 as the first of those violating American rights.

Resolved. That the following acts of parliament are infringements and violations of the rights of the colonists; and that the repeal of them is essentially necessary in order to restore harmony between

Great Britain and the American colonies, viz.

The several acts of 4 Geo. III. ch. 15, and [later acts] . . . which impose duties for the purpose of raising a revenue in America . . . are subversive of American rights.

Later, in almost an echo of Burke's "opened a new principle," the Congress called the taxation "a memorable change in the treatment of these Colonies."[22]

The parliamentary resolve in March 1764 to "charge certain Stamp Duties" revealed British intent to tax the colonies. The American protests of 1764—petitions, essays, and other writings—marked the beginning of the American Revolution. The protests not only asserted that Parliament had no authority to levy such taxes, they began an examination of the constitutional relationship between the colonies and Great Britain—an examination that began before passage of the Stamp Act in 1765.

A less obvious factor, but also marking the beginning of the revolution, was passage of the Sugar Act of 1764. The Sugar Act was not immediately recognized as being subversive of American rights, but colonial sensitivity to taxation grew over time. With mounting realization that port duties were taxes, it became clear that the Sugar Act was the starting point for a new British policy with regard to America. Eventually, Americans declared that repeal of the Sugar Act was necessary in order to restore harmony between Great Britain and the colonies.

The actions taken by the British government, and the American reaction that prompted the sequence of events ending in American independence, made 1764 the first year of the American Revolution.

NOTES

PREFACE

1. *The Parliamentary History of England, From the Earliest Period to the Year 1803*, vol. 17, *AD 1771–1774* (London: Printed by T. C. Hansard, 1813), 1241.
2. R. C. Simmons and P. D. G. Thomas, eds., *Proceedings and Debates of the British Parliaments Respecting North America, 1754--1783*, vol. 1, *1754--1764* (Millwood, NY: Kraus International, 1982), 494.
3. *Parliamentary History of England*, 17:1244.

INTRODUCTION

1. As a consequence of levying taxes on America, "Parliament and the colonial assemblies" were set on a "collision course." The collision became apparent, "When Parliament made the attempt with the program of direct taxation that began with the Sugar Act of 1764 [and the Stamp Act]." Edmund S. Morgan, *The Genuine Article: A Historian Looks at Early America* (New York: W. W. Norton, 2004), 190.
2. *The Parliamentary History of England, From the Earliest Period to the Year 1803*, vol. 16, *A. D. 1765–1771* (London: Printed by T.C. Hansard, 1813), 140-11.
3. Bernard Bailyn, ed., *Pamphlets of the American Revolution, 1750–1776: Vol. 1, 1750–1765* (Cambridge, MA: Belknap Press of Harvard University Press, 1965), 1:379.
4. Of course, eventually Americans saw that the Sugar Act was taxation and that British levy of duties for the purpose of revenue in 1764 constituted a change in colonial policy. The First Continental Congress, writing in October 1774, made the situation clear. The new policy was "a memorable change in the treatment of these Colonies." And further, "The present unhappy situation of our affairs is occasioned by a ruinous system of colony administration, adopted by the British ministry about the year 1763." See *Journals of the American Congress from 1774–1788: in four volumes* (Washington, DC: Way and Gideon, 1823), 1:23, 32.
5. P. D. G. Thomas, ed., "Parliamentary Diaries of Nathaniel Ryder, 1764–7," *Camden Miscellany, Vol. 23*, Camden Society, 4th series (London: Royal Historical Society, 1969), 7:256-57. By internal duty he was referring to stamp duties; by external duty he was referring to customs duties, "taxing the imports and exports."

6. The crux of the problem dealt with by the protests and essays was how "to allocate authority in such a way as to preserve the British rights of colonists in the distant polities in America while providing a measure of central direction for the empire as a whole." Confrontation of the question "in a sustained and systematic way, between 1764 and 1776," led to the development of "radically divergent views that ultimately led to the secession of thirteen of the North American colonies from the empire." Jack P. Greene, *The Constitutional Origins of the American Revolution* (New York: Cambridge University Press, 2011), 187.

7. "Taxation was to be the anvil on which the Anglo-American relationship broke." Peter D. G. Thomas, *Revolution in America: Britain and the Colonies, 1763–1776* (Cardiff: University of Wales Press, 1992), 15. Taxation was not a simple matter; it led to the dominating issues of the next decade: the supremacy of Parliament, and British sovereignty over the colonies. Of course, taxation was not the only problem. "The colonists had been brought to the brink of rebellion by a number of . . . provocative British measures from 1759 to 1764." There were eight "chief causes of colonial discontent," ending with the "serious and far-reaching … [Sugar Act] of 1764." Bernhard Knollenberg, *Origin of the American Revolution: 1759–1766* (New York: Macmillan, 1960), 1-3.

8. "It was direct parliamentary taxation of the colonies after 1763 that began the final dispute between Britain and the American colonies." And taxation led to an even more important issue. "The overriding constitutional issue of the age was the precise status of the colonial governments within the British Empire, and ultimately, the relationship between the British legislature and the colonial legislatures." Commentary by Merrill Jensen, in Randolph G. Adams, *Political Ideas of the American Revolution*, 3rd ed. (New York: Barnes & Noble, 1958), 19.

PROLOGUE

1. For further discussion of the economics of this trade, see Frank Wesley Pitman, *The Development of the British West Indies, 1700–1763* (New Haven, CT: Archon Books, 1917).

2. In contemporary writing, the act was known as the Sugar Act. In modern discourse (and on and off in 1763 and 1764), it is known as the Molasses Act. For more background on the genesis of the act and the surrounding controversy, see Albert B. Southwick, "The Molasses Act—Source of Precedents," *William and Mary Quarterly* 8, no. 3 (1951): 389-405, and Ken Shumate, "The Molasses Act: A Brief History," in *Journal of the American Revolution: Annual Volume 2020*, ed. Don N. Hagist (Yardley, PA: Westholme Publishing, 2020), 8–20.

3. Danby Pickering, *Statutes at Large* (Cambridge, UK: Printed by Joseph Bentham, 1765), 16:374-379 (quotations, 374). I have added italics to these and to other quotations throughout the book.

4. Hard currency was always in short supply in the colonies, a chronic problem since they required specie for the purchase of manufactured goods from Great Britain.

5. The import prohibition had the practical effect of prohibiting exports as well,

since the only payment French and Dutch planters would make for the American products was molasses (and sugar).

6. *Cobbett's Parliamentary History of England, from the Norman Conquest, in 1066, to the Year 1803, AD 1722–1733* (London: Printed by T. C. Hansard, 1811), 8:1262-63, 1266. Winnington's claim about the "custom always observed" overstated the case. However, this upholding of the refusal to hear petitions became "the precedent of 8 March 1733."

7. *Parliamentary History of England,* 17:1235.

8. John Lind, *Remarks on the Principal Acts of the Thirteenth Parliament of Great Britain* (London: Printed for T. Payne, 1775), 1:219.

PART ONE: BEFORE TAXATION

1. "The old English Colonial system—by which is generally meant the various provisions regulating the trade of the Empire," consisted of about one hundred parliamentary statutes. "The primary object of the colonial system was to develop the wealth and power of the Empire." George Louis Beer, *British Colonial Policy, 1754–1765* (New York: Macmillan, 1907), 193.

2. An American agent reported in early 1765, "The only reason why America has not been heretofore taxed in the fullest Manner, has been merely on Account of their Infancy and Inability." *Collections of the Connecticut Historical Society, The Fitch Papers, Vol. 2: January 1759–May 1766* (Hartford, CT: The Society, 1920), 18:319.

CHAPTER 1: A NEW COLONIAL POLICY

1. Indeed, it is fair to say, "The motivation behind the reforms in the Old Colonial System instituted by the British government after 1763 is difficult to assess." In fact, it is impossible to make "a definitive statement concerning the origins of the changes in imperial policy." Thomas C. Barrow, "A Project for Imperial Reform," *William and Mary Quarterly* (hereafter *WMQ*) 24, no. 1 (1967): 108-26 (quotations, 108).

2. Oliver M. Dickerson, *The Navigation Acts and the American Revolution* (New Haven, CT: Yale University Press, 1951), xiv. Dickerson further characterizes these decisions as "a revolution in the century-old trade and navigation system."

3. Stamp duties were excise taxes placed on transactions internal to the commerce of the colonies. Legal papers and other printed documents were to be taxed; revenue stamps were used to demonstrate that the tax had been paid.

4. John Shy, *Toward Lexington: The Role of the British Army in the Coming of the American Revolution* (Princeton, NJ: Princeton University Press, 1965), especially chap. 2, "The Decision of 1763" (quotation, 45). There were also political considerations for retention of a large peacetime army in America.

5. For more information on the extensive enforcement actions taking place, see John L. Bullion, *A Great and Necessary Measure: George Grenville and the Genesis of the Stamp Act* (Columbia: University of Missouri Press, 1982). See especially chap. 4, "'The First Great Object': Obstructing the Clandestine Trade to America."

6. This was a major effort; Charles Andrews discusses the "mass of evidence and these many recommendations" analyzed by the Treasury, resulting in "a very important paper—one of the most so of this critical period." Charles M. Andrews, *The Colonial Period of American History* (New Haven, CT: Yale University Press, 1938), 4:219. John Bullion discusses this issue at length in *Great and Necessary Measure*, chap. 5, "Taxing Molasses, July 1763–March 1764."

7. James Munro, ed., *Acts of the Privy Council of England: Colonial Series, AD 1745–1766* (London: His Majesty's Stationery Office, 1911), 4:569. The Order in Council quotes in its entirety the Grenville report of the previous day. For detail on the fateful decisions being made in London at this time, see Thomas C. Barrow, "Background to the Grenville Program, 1757–1763," *WMQ* 22, no. 1 (1965): 93-104.

8. Grenville's program extended beyond revenue. "The British barrage of legislation for the colonies in 1764 was unprecedented." As a consequence, "If any one year was the starting point of the prerevolutionary era, [1764] has the best claim to the title." Theodore Draper, *A Struggle for Power: The American Revolution* (New York: Times Books, 1996), 209. "The Sugar Act of 1764, not the Stamp Act of 1765, first brought out the colonial threat to British manufactures." Ibid., 334.

9. The decision, and preparation of an act, to impose stamp duties started in July. See Bullion, *Great and Necessary Measure*, 104-10. In fact, the measure that was great and necessary was the 1765 Stamp Act, necessary in order to establish the right of Parliament to impose taxes on the colonies.

10. *Jasper Mauduit: Agent in London for the Province of the Massachusetts-Bay 1762–1765* (Boston: Massachusetts Historical Society Collections, 1918), 74:101, 159.

11. George Bancroft, *History of the United States, from the Discovery of the American Continent* (Boston: Little, Brown, 1875), 5:88n.

12. Colin Nicolson, ed., *The Papers of Francis Bernard: Governor of Colonial Massachusetts, 1760–69, Vol. 1: 1759–1763* (Boston: Colonial Society of Massachusetts, 2007), 73:381-82. The editor of the Bernard papers comments, "This is the first official notification that Francis Bernard and the other governors received of Britain's intention to reinvigorate the mercantlist system by improving both enforcement of the trade laws and revenue collection. The ensuing controversy is traditionally regarded as the onset of the imperial crisis that presaged the Revolution."

13. A great deal of the most insightful colonial correspondence in 1764 consists of letters to and from Richard Jackson. He was an attorney, member of Parliament, and widely known as an unusually knowledgeable man—"omniscient Jackson" he was called. His additional role as a secretary to Grenville gave him substantial influence to support America but also had potential for a conflict of interest. Benjamin Franklin characterized him as "the best acquainted with our American affairs and constitutions, as well as with government law in general [and] also thoroughly knowing in the present views of the Board of Trade, and in their connexions and characters."

14. John W. Tyler and Elizabeth Dubrulle, eds., *The Correspondence of Thomas Hutchinson, Vol. 1: 1740–1766* (Boston: Colonial Society of Massachusetts, 2014), 84:182.

15. Nicolson, ed., *Papers of Francis Bernard*, 73:426.

16. Ibid., 73:428

17. Ibid., 73:420-21.

18. Ibid., 73:447-49.

19. Leonard W. Labaree, ed., *The Papers of Benjamin Franklin* (New Haven, CT: Yale University Press, 1966), 10:415.

20. Tricky indeed. Among many uses of taxation as a synonym for customs duty is this statement from then Prime Minister Lord North, "Very often the best method of regulating commerce is by taxation." Lord North is at this time proposing conciliation with America in Parliament. *London Chronicle*, February 25, 1775, quoted in Thomas, *Revolution in America,* 78. This is in the context of a tax defined as a payment required to be made for imperial purposes, for the benefit of the entire community.

21. *Collections of the Massachusetts Historical Society for the Year 1798* (Boston, 1798), 6:193.

22. Leonard W. Labaree, ed., *The Papers of Benjamin Franklin* (New Haven, CT: Yale University Press, 1967), 11:34-35.

23. Nicolson, ed., *Papers of Francis Bernard*, 73:432.

24. Lawrence Henry Gipson, *The Triumphant Empire: Thunder-Clouds Gather in the West, 1763–1766*, The British Empire before the American Revolution (New York: Knopf, 1961), 10:209.

25. Colin Nicolson, ed., *The Papers of Francis Bernard: Governor of Colonial Massachusetts, 1760–69, Vol. 2: 1764–1765* (Boston: Colonial Society of Massachusetts, 2012), 81:29.

CHAPTER 2: AMERICA PROTESTS ENFORCEMENT

1. This chapter has been adapted from Ken Shumate, "Reasons against the Renewal of the Sugar Act," *Journal of the American Revolution*, June 4, 11, and 18, 2020.

2. Charles M. Andrews, "The Boston Merchants and the Non-importation Movement," *Publications of the Colonial Society of Massachusetts,* vol. 19, *Transactions, 1916–1917* (Boston, 1918), 159-259 (quotations, 161, 166). Later reports justified the fear of renewal, but shortly after organization the merchants learned that the duties were put off for a year.

3. *Journals of the House of Representatives of Massachusetts: 1763–1764* (Boston: Massachusetts Historical Society, 1970), 40:132.

4. As appalling as was the slavery in the West Indies, the slave trade and treatment of slaves must be addressed as an integral part of eighteenth-century commerce. "Slavery is of course fundamental to the history of the eighteenth-century West Indies." The islands' wealth was based on "the ruthless exploitation of a labour force of some half a million enslaved Africans and their constant replenishment by new imports." P. J. Marshall, *Edmund Burke and the British Empire in the West Indies: Wealth, Power, and Slavery* (Oxford: Oxford University Press, 2019), 2.

5. Charles M. Andrews, "State of the Trade, 1763," *Publications of the Colonial Society of Massachusetts,* vol. 19, *Transactions, 1916–1917* (Boston, 1918), 379-90 (quotations, 382-90). The memorial and the later reasons against the renewal from other colonies were to some extent simply bits of puffery, exaggerating the likely effect of the high tariff on molasses.

6. Ibid., 19:380-81.

7. *Reasons against the renewal of the Sugar Act as it will be prejudicial to the trade, not only of the northern colonies, but to that of Great-Britain also* (Boston: Province of the Massachusetts-Bay, 1764), 2, 19.

8. Nicolson, ed., *Papers of Francis Bernard,* 81:52-53.

9. Robert J. Taylor, "Israel Mauduit," *New England Quarterly* 24, no. 2 (1951): 208-30.

10. Merrill Jensen, ed., *Tracts of the American Revolution, 1763–1776* (Indianapolis: Bobbs-Merrill, 1966), 3-18.

11. *Monthly Review, or Literary Journal* (London: Printed for R. Griffiths, at the Dunciad in St. Paul's Church-yard, 1764), 30:464-66.

12. Nicolson, ed., *Papers of Francis Bernard,* 81:53.

13. Frederick Bernays Wiener, "The Rhode Island Merchants and the Sugar Act," *New England Quarterly* 3, no. 3 (1930): 464-500 (quotation, 473-74).

14. John Russell Bartlett, ed., *Records of the Colony of Rhode Island and Providence Plantations, in New England: 1757–1769* (Providence: By Order of the General Assembly, 1861), 6:378-83.

15. Wiener, "Rhode Island Merchants," 492-93.

16. Lawrence Henry Gipson, *Jared Ingersoll: A Study of American Loyalism in Relation to British Colonial Government* (New Haven, CT: Yale University Press, and London: Oxford University Press, 1920), 113. Gipson also discusses related actions of the merchants and the Assembly.

17. *The Fitch Papers,* 18:275-79.

18. Andrews, "Boston Merchants," 19:166n. Pennsylvania played little role in the organized protest as the province was embroiled in a controversy over a proposed change in government from proprietary to royal.

19. *Journal of the Votes and Proceedings of the General Assembly of the Colony of New-York. Began the 8th Day of November, 1743; and Ended the 23d of December, 1765.* Published by Order of the General Assembly (New York, 1766), 2:740-44.

20. Knollenberg, *Origin of the American Revolution,* 148.

21. Thomas Whately, *The Regulations Lately Made Concerning the Colonies, and the Taxes Imposed Upon Them, Considered* (London: Printed for J. Wilkie, 1765), 104-5.

22. Bailyn, ed., *Pamphlets,* 1:467-68.

23. Richard Price, *Observations on the Nature of Civil Liberty, the Principles of Government, and the Justice and Policy of the War with America* (London: Printed for T. Cadell, 1776), 25.

24. *Jasper Mauduit: Agent in London,* 74:145-46.

25. *Collections of the Massachusetts Historical Society for the Year 1798,* 6:193.

26. Bailyn, ed., *Pamphlets,* 1:358-59.

PART TWO: TAXATION

1. Tyler and Dubrulle, eds., *Correspondence of Thomas Hutchinson*, 84:212. He requested that Jackson not reveal that this was Hutchinson's opinion.
2. "It was the serious attempt by the British government [to enforce the Molasses Act], and again in 1764, by lower duties [i.e., the renewal], to interfere with trade to the foreign West Indies, that ushered in the revolutionary movement." Pitman, *Development*, 272.

CHAPTER 3: THE SUGAR ACT

1. *The Parliamentary History of England, From the Earliest Period to the Year 1803*, vol. 15, A. D. 1753–1765 (London: Printed by T.C. Hansard, 1813), 1337, 1340.
2. Peter D. G. Thomas, *British Politics and the Stamp Act Crisis: The First Phase of the American Revolution, 1763–1767* (Oxford: Clarendon Press, 1975), 52-53.
3. Simmons and Thomas, eds., *Proceedings*, 487-95.
4. See Edmund S. Morgan and Helen M. Morgan, *The Stamp Act Crisis: Prologue to Revolution* (Chapel Hill: University of North Carolina Press, 1953), and Thomas, *British Politics*.
5. Reports of the discussion on this topic gave varied reasons for the postponement, "and the subsequent misrepresentation of them reveal something of the confusion, misunderstanding, and duplicity which plagued Anglo-American relations in the period leading up to the Revolution." Edmund S. Morgan, "The Postponement of the Stamp Act," *WMQ* 7, no. 3 (1950): 353-92 (quotation, 355).
6. *Parliamentary History of England*, 15:1434.
7. Beer, *British Colonial Policy*, 277.
8. Bailyn, *Pamphlets*, 1:356.
9. All Sugar Act quotations are from Pickering, *Statutes at Large*, 26:33-52 (quotations, 33-37, 49).
10. For more about the Sugar Act, see Allen S. Johnson, "The Passage of the Sugar Act," *WMQ* 16, no. 4 (1959): 507-14, and Ken Shumate, "The Sugar Act: A Brief History," *Journal of the American Revolution*, September 17, 2018.
11. William Allen and Lewis Burd Walker, *Extracts from Chief Justice William Allen's Letter Book* (Pottsville, PA: Standard, 1897), 65. Allen was not the only American to comment on interference with intercolonial commerce. In chapter ten we will see a letter in which Benjamin Franklin complains that "the Men of War station'd in our several Ports are very active in their new Employment of Custom house Officers; a Portmanteau cannot go between here [Philadelphia] and New York without being search'd."
12. Morgan, "Postponement," 357.
13. *Jasper Mauduit: Agent in London*, 74:147n.
14. Gipson, *Triumphant Empire*, 10:231.
15. Todd Andrlik, *Reporting the Revolutionary War: Before It Was History, It Was News* (Naperville, IL: Sourcebooks, 2012), 4.

16. Whately, *Regulations Lately Made*, 87-88. This 114-page pamphlet was at first attributed to George Grenville. It was little short of an official statement of the government, serving as an explanation and defense of the actions taken by Parliament in 1764.
17. *Journals of the American Congress*, 1:21.
18. *Parliamentary History of England*, 17:1235-42.
19. *Parliamentary History of England*, 16:144, 148-49, 159.
20. Thomas, *Camden Miscellany*, 7:302.
21. *Journals of the American Congress*, 1:21.

CHAPTER 4: NOTIFICATION OF STAMP DUTIES

1. *Jasper Mauduit: Agent in London*, 74:147n.
2. Ninetta S. Jucker, ed., *The Jenkinson Papers, 1760–1766* (London: Macmillan, 1949), 305.
3. Nicolson, ed., *Papers of Francis Bernard*, 81:113-14.
4. *Fitch Papers*, 18:296-97.
5. Massachusetts Historical Society, 6th ser., *The Bowdoin and Temple Papers* (Boston: The Society, 1897), 9:22.
6. Franklin B. Dexter, ed., "A Selection from the Correspondence and Miscellaneous Papers of Jared Ingersoll," *Papers of the New Haven Colony Historical Society* (New Haven, CT: The Society, 1918), 9:201-472 (quotation, 293-95).
7. Ibid., 295-300.
8. Massachusetts Historical Society, *Bowdoin and Temple Papers*, 9:20.
9. Ibid., 9:24-26.

PART THREE: PROTESTS

1. Contrariwise, Edmund Morgan has made an influential but controversial argument that the colonies did not acquiesce to external taxation in 1764. See Edmund S. Morgan, "Colonial Ideas of Parliamentary Power 1764–1766," *WMQ* 5, no. 3 (1948): 311-41. For an overview and analysis of Morgan's position, see Eric Nelson, *The Royalist Revolution: Monarchy and the American Founding* (Cambridge, MA: Harvard University Press, 2014), 32, and especially note 10.
2. Greene, *Constitutional Origins*, 67, 68.
3. Petitions and essays were not the only form of objection to the new Grenville program. A protest movement against stamp duties that did not quite get off the ground in 1764 (worthy of mention here since it became important in 1765) was that of *nonimportation*, a boycott of British manufactured goods. "Upon the news of the intention to lay this duty on the colonies, many people," reported Thomas Hutchinson, had formed associations "engaged to forbear the importation, or consumption, of English goods." He reported, "This was intended to alarm the manufacturers in England." Thomas Hutchinson, *The history of the province of Massachusetts Bay: from 1749 to 1774* (London: J. Murray, 1828), 3:116-17. The plan was batted about in a number of colonies but never reached a threatening level. A related threat, also coming up from time to time and place to place, was the threat of *local manufacture*, the intent to produce products locally in place of importation from Britain.

4. The interrelationship between these pamphlets, and their relation to other writings, is discussed at length in Bailyn, ed., *Pamphlets*.

CHAPTER 5: NEW YORK

1. *General Assembly of the Colony of New-York*, 2:749-50.
2. Charles Z. Lincoln, ed., *Messages from the Governors, 1683–1776, Colonial Period* (Albany, NY: J. B. Lyon, 1909), 1:684.
3. *General Assembly of the Colony of New-York*, 2:754.
4. *The Colden Letter Books, Vol. 1: 1760–1765* (New York: Printed for the New York Historical Society, 1877), 9:362-64.
5. Merrill Jensen, *The Founding of a Nation: A History of the American Revolution* (New York: Oxford University Press, 1968), 94.
6. All three petitions are in *General Assembly of the Colony of New-York*, 2:769-79.
7. *Fitch Papers*, 18:335. This was Jared Ingersoll writing Governor Fitch on March 6, 1765.

CHAPTER 6: MASSACHUSETTS

1. *A Report of the Record Commissioners of the City of Boston, Containing the Boston Town Records, 1758 to 1769* (Boston: Rockwell and Churchill, 1886), 121-22, reprinted in *American Colonial Documents to 1776, English Historical Documents*, ed. Merrill Jensen (London: Eyre & Spottiswoode, 1955), 9:663-64.
2. *Journals of the House of Representatives of Massachusetts: 1764–1765* (Boston: Massachusetts Historical Society, 1971), 41:14.
3. Ibid., 41:72-77.
4. Hutchinson, *history of the province*, 3:110.
5. Massachusetts Historical Society, *Proceedings of the Massachusetts Historical Society* (Boston: Massachusetts Historical Society, 1875), 13:189-90.
6. Nicolson, ed., *Papers of Francis Bernard*, 81:90.
7. Letter to William Tudor, August 21, 1818. See Charles Francis Adams, ed., *The Works of John Adams, Second President of the United States* (Boston: Little, Brown, 1856), 10:351. Otis's later career was checkered: confused and contradictory, denying some key ideas of his early writing.
8. James Otis, *The Rights of the British Colonies Asserted and Proved* (Boston, 1764) as reprinted in Bailyn, ed., *Pamphlets*, 1:474-82.
9. The pamphlet is lengthy and addresses a number of broad constitutional topics. I present only extracts particularly relevant to the taxation issues and the Sugar Act. For further analysis, see Bailyn, ed., *Pamphlets*, 1:409-17. Bailyn is supportive of Otis's arguments, finding complexity but not ambiguity in the intricate rationale.
10. Incidentally, Otis had earlier in the essay inveighed against black slavery, asserting, "The colonists are by the law of nature freeborn, as indeed all men are, white or black." And against slavers: "It is a clear truth that those who every day barter away other men's liberty will soon care little for their own." He also deplored the situation of women, declaiming, "Are not women born as free as men? Would it not be infamous to assert that the ladies are all slaves by nature?"

11. Bailyn, ed., *Pamphlets*, 1:418-82. Also see Gordon S. Wood, ed., *The American Revolution: Writings from the Pamphlet Debate 1764–1776* (New York: Library of America, 2015), 1:41-119.

12. John Philip Reid, *The Authority to Tax*, vol. 2 of *Constitutional History of the American Revolution* (Madison: University of Wisconsin Press, 1987), 206.

13. Although not as important for the story of 1764 as the taxation aspects of the Sugar Act, these regulations "threatened in themselves to revolutionize the traditionally loose administrative relationship between England and America. But they threatened more. They raised issues of constitutionalism, of individual rights, and of the administration of justice; and they raised, also, profoundly disquieting suspicions of the motivations of the people responsible for such legislation in England." Bailyn, ed., *Pamphlets*, 1:484.

14. Bailyn, ed., *Pamphlets*, 1:490-98.

15. *Novanglus, And Massachusettensis; Or, Political Essays, Published in the Years 1774 And 1775* (Boston: Hews & Goss, 1819), 100. This was letter 8, of March 13, 1775. Also see Charles Francis Adams, ed., *The Works of John Adams, Second President of the United States* (Boston: Little, Brown, 1851), 4:129.

16. Massachusetts Historical Society, *Proceedings of the Massachusetts Historical Society*, 20:49-52.

17. Alden Bradford, ed., *Speeches of the Governors of Massachusetts from 1765 to 1775* (Boston: Printed by Russell and Gardner, 1818, republished, New York: Da Capo Press, 1971), 21-23.

18. Hutchinson, *history of the province*, 3:114.

19. Tyler and Dubrulle, eds., *Correspondence of Thomas Hutchinson*, 84:404.

20. Nicolson, ed., *Papers of Francis Bernard*, 81:161-66.

21. Tyler and Dubrulle, eds., *Correspondence of Thomas Hutchinson*, 84:239-40.

22. Bradford, *Speeches of the Governors*, 24-25.

23. *Jasper Mauduit: Agent in London*, 74:167-69.

24. Ibid., 74:170-71.

25. Ibid., 74:171-79.

26. Bradford, *Speeches of the Governors*, 28-29.

CHAPTER 7: VIRGINIA

1. Richard H. Lee (the younger), *Memoir of the life of Richard H. Lee, and his Correspondence with the most distinguished Men in America and Europe* (Philadelphia: Carey and Lea, 1825), 1:27-29.

2. Virginia Historical Society, "Proceedings of the Virginia Committee of Correspondence, 1759–1767," *Virginia Magazine of History and Biography* (hereafter *VMHB*) 12, no. 1 (1904): 1-14 (quotation, 8-13).

3. Virginia Historical Society, "Virginia Legislative Documents (continued)," *VMHB* 10, no. 1 (1902): 1-16 (quotation, 3-4).

4. Virginia Historical Society, *VMHB* 12, no. 1 (1904): 13.

5. Bailyn, ed., *Pamphlets*, 1:319-24.

6. Jensen, ed., *Tracts of the American Revolution*, 117. Also, Wood, ed., *American Revolution*, 1:321.

7. Greene, *Constitutional Origins*, 82.

8. John Pendleton Kennedy, ed., *Journals of the House of Burgesses of Virginia, 1761–1765* (Richmond: Library Board of the State of Virginia, 1907), 10:256-57.

9. Ibid., 10:302-4.

10. Virginia Historical Society, "Virginia Legislative Documents," *VMHB* 9, no. 4 (1902): 353-68 (quotation, 354-55).

11. Kennedy, ed., *Journals of the House*, 10:lviii.

12. L. B. Namier, "Charles Garth, Agent for South Carolina: Part 2 (Continued)," *English Historical Review* 54, no. 216 (1939): 632–52 (quotation, 650). Garth wrote to South Carolina on February 17, 1765.

13. E. J. Miller, "The Virginia Legislature and the Stamp Act," *WMQ* 21, no. 4 (1913): 233–48 (quotation 245).

CHAPTER 8: CONNECTICUT

1. Ebenezer Silliman was a councilman and George Wyllys was a member of the assembly. Jared Ingersoll was not in government but was a particularly important lawyer in the colony. "Although not a member of the assembly, Jared Ingersoll was asked to serve on this committee. . . . The mere fact that the assembly went outside of the governmental circle to procure Ingersoll's services would seem to indicate a feeling that, by reason of his eminence as an advocate and on account of his experience as London agent, he was peculiarly qualified to marshal against the ministerial plan the most effective arguments." Gipson, *Jared Ingersoll*, 124.

2. *The Public Records of the Colony of Connecticut [1636–1776]* (Hartford, CT: Press of the Case, 1890), 9:256.

3. Fitch was not alone in proposing specific items appropriate to be taxed for the sake of raising a revenue. For example, in February, Benjamin Franklin had written Richard Jackson, "If Money must be raised from us to support 14 Battallions, as you mention, I think ... a moderate Duty on Foreign Mellasses may be collected; when a high one could not. The same on foreign Wines; and a Duty not only on Tea, but on all East India Goods might perhaps not be amiss, as they are generally rather Luxuries than Necessaries." Labaree, ed., *Papers of Benjamin Franklin*, 11:76.

4. Connecticut General Assembly, *Public Records of the Colony*, 9:653-671. Also, Bailyn, ed., *Pamphlets*, 1:386-407.

5. Tyler and Dubrulle, eds., *Correspondence of Thomas Hutchinson*, 84:237-38.

6. *Fitch Papers*, 18:303-305.

CHAPTER 9: RHODE ISLAND

1. An earlier event, one that provides a backdrop to the story of Rhode Island, has to do with the enforcement of the laws of trade. A side effect of the presence of the Royal Navy in American waters was the impressment of local sailors to fill out ships' crews. In July, the British armed schooner *St. John* had a confrontation with the residents and officials of Newport. This is only one of many confrontations between the colonies and the Royal Navy in late 1763 and 1764,

but the noteworthy conclusion to this affair was that on July 9, a Rhode Island artillery battery fired on the *St. John* as it departed Newport harbor against the orders of local officials. One of the shots fired pierced the mainsail of the *St. John*. Americans were cannonading the Royal Navy! The resulting diplomatic controversy between colonial officials and the Board of Trade extended for over a year, until more-important events regarding the Stamp Act shoved this uproar into the background.

2. Bartlett, ed., *Records of the Colony of Rhode Island*, 6:403-4.

3. *Fitch Papers*, 18:290-91.

4. Bartlett, ed., *Records of the Colony of Rhode Island*, 6:411.

5. Ibid., 6:414-16.

6. Ibid., 6:416-27; Bailyn, ed., *Pamphlets*, 1:507-22.

7. Gertrude S. Kimball, ed., *The Correspondence of the Colonial Governors of Rhode Island 1723–1775* (New York: Houghton, Mifflin, 1902), 2:361-62.

CHAPTER 10: OTHER AMERICAN COLONIES

1. Labaree, ed., *Papers of Benjamin Franklin*, 11:181, 215.

2. Ibid., 11:348-51.

3. Frederick W. Ricord and Wm. Nelson, eds., *Documents Relating to the Colonial History of the State of New Jersey* (Newark: New Jersey Historical Society, 1885), 9:449-50.

4. Knollenberg, *Origin of the American Revolution*, 214.

5. William L. Saunders, ed., *The Colonial Records of North Carolina* (Raleigh: Joseph Daniels, 1888), 6:1260-61.

6. Jack P. Greene, *The Quest for Power: The Lower Houses of Assembly in the Southern Royal Colonies, 1689–1776* (New York: W. W. Norton, 1972; copyright 1963, University of North Carolina Press), 365.

7. R. W. Gibbes, *Documentary History of the American Revolution, 1764–1776* (New York: D. Appleton, 1855), 2-5.

8. Namier, "Charles Garth," 648-49.

9. Ibid., 651.

EPILOGUE

1. Andrlik, *Reporting the Revolutionary War*, 7.

2. "Journal, December 1764: Vol. 71," in *Journals of the Board of Trade and Plantations: Vol. 12, January 1764–December 1767*, ed. K. H. Ledward (London: His Majesty's Stationery Office, 1936), 120-31; *British History Online*, accessed October 5, 2020, http://www.british-history.ac.uk/jrnl-trade-plantations/vol12/pp120-131.

3. E. B. O'Callaghan, ed., *Documents relative to the colonial history of the State of New-York; procured in Holland, England, and France* (Albany: New York State Legislature, 1856), 7:678.

4. Munro, ed., *Acts of the Privy Council*, 4:692.

5. William James Smith, ed., *The Grenville papers: being the correspondence of Richard Grenville, earl Temple, K.G., and the right Hon. George Grenville, their friends and contemporaries* (London: John Murray, 1852), 2:478.

6. Bullion, *Great and Necessary Measure*, 225.

7. Massachusetts Historical Society, *Bowdoin and Temple Papers,* 9:37.

8. Ibid., 9:49.

9. *Tenth Report of the Royal Commission on Historical Manuscripts* (London: H. M. Stationery Office, 1885), 382.

10. P. D. G. Thomas, *The House of Commons in the Eighteenth Century* (Oxford: Clarendon Press, 1971), 71.

11. Massachusetts Historical Society, *Bowdoin and Temple Papers*, 9:61.

12. Nicolson, ed., *Papers of Francis Bernard*, 81:413.

13. Jensen, *Founding of a Nation*, 331.

14. Thomas, ed., "Parliamentary Diaries," 7:344.

15. Massachusetts Historical Society, *Collections of the Massachusetts Historical Society, The Trumbull Papers* (Boston: published by the Society, 1885), 9:229.

16. William Dowdeswell letter to to the Marquis of Rockingham, August 14, 1768, in Warren M. Elofson, *The Rockingham Connection and the Second Founding of the Whig Party 1768–1773* (Montreal, QC, and Kingston, ON: McGill-Queen's University Press, 1996), 43.

17. Sir Henry Cavendish, *Sir Henry Cavendish's Debates of the House of commons, during the thirteenth Parliament of Great Britain, commonly called the unreported Parliament; to which are appended illustrations of the parliamentary history of the reign of George the Third; consisting of unpublished letters, private journals, memoirs, &c.* (London: Longman, Orme, Brown, Green, & Longmans [etc.], 1841), 1:213. This was in a debate of February 8, 1769.

18. Francis Bernard letter to Lord Barrington, January 28, 1768, in *The Papers of Francis Bernard: Governor of Colonial Massachusetts, 1760–69, Vol. 4: 1768,* ed. Colin Nicolson (Boston: Colonial Society of Massachusetts, 2015), 86:83.

19. Gordon S. Wood, *The Creation of the American Republic, 1776–1787* (Chapel Hill: University of North Carolina Press, 1969), 349.

20. *Parliamentary History of England*, 17:1218.

21. Ibid., 17:1241.

22. *Journals of the American Congress*, 1:19, 21, 32.

BIBLIOGRAPHY

BOOKS

Adams, Charles Francis, ed. *The Works of John Adams, Second President of the United States.* Vol. 4. Boston: Little, Brown, 1851.

———. *The Works of John Adams, Second President of the United States.* Vol. 10. Boston: Little, Brown, 1856.

Adams, Randolph G. *Political Ideas of the American Revolution.* 3rd ed. New York: Barnes & Noble, 1958.

Allen, William, and Lewis Burd Walker. *Extracts from Chief Justice William Allen's Letter Book.* Vol. 65. Pottsville, PA: Standard Publishing, 1897.

Andrews, Charles M. "The Boston Merchants and the Non-importation Movement." In *Publications of the Colonial Society of Massachusetts: Transactions, 1916–1917.* Vol. 19, 159-259. Boston, 1918.

———. *The Colonial Period of American History.* Vol. 4. New Haven, CT: Yale University Press, 1938.

———. "State of the Trade, 1763." In *Publications of the Colonial Society of Massachusetts: Transactions, 1916–1917.* Vol. 19, 379-90. Boston, 1918.

Andrlik, Todd. *Reporting the Revolutionary War: Before It Was History, It Was News.* Vol. 4. Naperville, IL: Sourcebooks, 2012.

Bailyn, Bernard, ed. *Pamphlets of the American Revolution, 1750–1776: Vol. 1, 1750–1765.* Cambridge, MA: Belknap Press of Harvard University Press, 1965.

Bancroft, George. *History of the United States, from the Discovery of the American Continent.* Vol. 5. Boston: Little, Brown, 1875.

Bartlett, John Russell, ed. *Records of the Colony of Rhode Island and Providence Plantations, in New England: 1757–1769.* Providence: By Order of the General Assembly, 1861.

Beer, George Louis. *British Colonial Policy, 1754–1765.* New York: Macmillan, 1907.

Bradford, Alden, ed. *Speeches of the Governors of Massachusetts from 1765 to 1775.* Boston: Printed by Russell and Gardner, 1818. Republished, New York: Da Capo Press, 1971.

Bullion, John L. *A Great and Necessary Measure: George Grenville and the Genesis of the Stamp Act.* Columbia: University of Missouri Press, 1982.

Cavendish, Henry. *Sir Henry Cavendish's Debates of the House of Commons, during the thirteenth Parliament of Great Britain, commonly called the unreported Parliament; to which are appended illustrations of the parliamentary history of the reign of George the Third; consisting of unpublished letters, private journals, memoirs, &c.* Vol. 1. London: Longman, Orme, Brown, Green, & Longmans [etc.], 1841.

Cobbett's Parliamentary History of England, from the Norman Conquest, in 1066, to the Year 1803. Vol. 8, AD 1722–1733. London: Printed by T. C. Hansard, 1811.

The Colden Letter Books, Vol. 1, 1760–1765. Vol. 9. New York: Printed for the New York Historical Society, 1877.

Collections of the Connecticut Historical Society, The Fitch Papers, Vol. 2: January 1759–May 1766. Vol. 18. Hartford, CT: The Society, 1920.

Collections of the Massachusetts Historical Society for the Year 1798. Vol. 6. Boston, 1798.

Dexter, Franklin B., ed. "A Selection from the Correspondence and Miscellaneous Papers of Jared Ingersoll." In *Papers of the New Haven Colony Historical Society.* Vol. 9, 201-472. New Haven, CT: The Society, 1918.

Dickerson, Oliver M. *The Navigation Acts and the American Revolution.* New Haven, CT: Yale University Press, 1951.

Draper, Theodore. *A Struggle for Power: The American Revolution.* New York: Times Books, 1996.

Elofson, Warren M. *The Rockingham Connection and the Second Founding of the Whig Party 1768–1773.* Montreal, QC, and Kingston, ON: McGill-Queen's University Press, 1996.

Gibbes, R. W. *Documentary History of the American Revolution, 1764–1776.* New York: D. Appleton, 1855.

Gipson, Lawrence Henry. *Jared Ingersoll: A Study of American Loyalism in Relation to British Colonial Government.* New Haven, CT: Yale University Press, and London: Oxford University Press, 1920.

———. *The Triumphant Empire: Thunder-Clouds Gather in the West, 1763–1766.* Vol. 10 of The British Empire before the American Revolution. New York: Knopf, 1961.

Greene, Jack P. *The Constitutional Origins of the American Revolution.* New York: Cambridge University Press, 2011.

———. *The Quest for Power: The Lower Houses of Assembly in the Southern Royal Colonies, 1689–1776.* New York: Norton, 1972. Copyright 1963 by the University of North Carolina Press.

Hutchinson, Thomas. *The history of the province of Massachusetts Bay: from 1749 to 1774.* Vol. 3. London: J. Murray, 1828.

Jasper Mauduit: Agent in London for the Province of the Massachusetts-Bay 1762–1765. Vol. 74. Boston: Massachusetts Historical Society Collections, 1918.

Jensen, Merrill. "Commentary." In Randolph G. Adams, *Political Ideas of the American Revolution,* 3rd ed. New York: Barnes & Noble, 1958.

———. *The Founding of a Nation: A History of the American Revolution.* New York: Oxford University Press, 1968.

———, ed. *American Colonial Documents to 1776, English Historical Documents.* Vol. 9. London: Eyre & Spottiswoode, 1955.

———, ed. *Tracts of the American Revolution, 1763–1776.* Vol. 3. Indianapolis: Bobbs-Merrill, 1966.

Journal of the Votes and Proceedings of the General Assembly of the Colony of New-York. Began the 8th Day of November, 1743; and Ended the 23d of December, 1765. Vol. 2. New York: Published by Order of the General Assembly, 1766.

Journals of the American Congress from 1774–1788: in four volumes. Vol. 1. Washington, DC: Printed and published by Way and Gideon, 1823.

Journals of the House of Representatives of Massachusetts: 1763–1764. Vol. 40. Boston: Massachusetts Historical Society, 1970.

Journals of the House of Representatives of Massachusetts: 1764–1765. Vol. 41. Boston: Massachusetts Historical Society, 1971.

Jucker, Ninetta S., ed., *The Jenkinson Papers, 1760–1766.* London: Macmillan, 1949.

Kennedy, John Pendleton, ed. *Journals of the House of Burgesses of Virginia, 1761–1765.* Vol. 10. Richmond: Library Board of the State of Virginia, 1907.

Kimball, Gertrude S., ed. *The Correspondence of the Colonial Governors of Rhode Island 1723–1775.* Vol. 2. New York: Houghton, Mifflin, 1902.

Knollenberg, Bernhard. *Origin of the American Revolution: 1759–1766.* New York: Macmillan, 1960.

Labaree, Leonard W., ed. *The Papers of Benjamin Franklin.* Vol. 10. New Haven, CT: Yale University Press, 1966.

———. *The Papers of Benjamin Franklin.* Vol. 11. New Haven, CT: Yale University Press, 1967.

Lee, Richard H. (the younger). *Memoir of the life of Richard H. Lee, and his Correspondence with the most distinguished Men in America and Europe.* Vol. 1. Philadelphia: Carey and Lea, 1825.

Lincoln, Charles Z., ed. *Messages from the Governors.* Vol. 1, *1683–1776, Colonial Period.* Albany, NY: J. B. Lyon, 1909.

Lind, John. *Remarks on the Principal Acts of the Thirteenth Parliament of Great Britain.* Vol. 1. London: Printed for T. Payne, 1775.

Marshall, P. J. *Edmund Burke and the British Empire in the West Indies: Wealth, Power, and Slavery.* Oxford: Oxford University Press, 2019.

Massachusetts Historical Society. *Proceedings of the Massachusetts Historical Society.* Vol. 20. Boston: Massachusetts Historical Society, 1884.

———. *Collections of the Massachusetts Historical Society, The Trumbull Papers.* Vol. 9. Boston: Massachusetts Historical Society, 1885.

———. *Proceedings of the Massachusetts Historical Society.* Vol. 13. Boston: Massachusetts Historical Society, 1875.

———. 6th ser. *The Bowdoin and Temple Papers.* Vol. 9. Boston: Massachusetts Historical Society, 1897.

Monthly Review, or Literary Journal. Vol. 30. London: Printed for R. Griffiths, at the Dunciad in St. Paul's Church-yard, 1764.

Morgan, Edmund S. *The Genuine Article: A Historian Looks at Early America.* New York: W. W. Norton, 2004.

Morgan, Edmund S., and Helen M. Morgan. *The Stamp Act Crisis: Prologue to Revolution.* Chapel Hill: University of North Carolina Press, 1953.

Munro, James, ed. *Acts of the Privy Council of England: Colonial Series, AD 1745–1766.* Vol. 4. London: His Majesty's Stationery Office, 1911.

Nelson, Eric. *The Royalist Revolution: Monarchy and the American Founding.* Cambridge, MA: Harvard University Press, 2014.

Nicolson, Colin, ed. *The Papers of Francis Bernard: Governor of Colonial Massachusetts, 1760–69, Vol. 1: 1759–1763.* Vol. 73. Boston: Colonial Society of Massachusetts, 2007.

———. *The Papers of Francis Bernard: Governor of Colonial Massachusetts, 1760–69, Vol. 2: 1764–1765.* Vol. 81. Boston: Colonial Society of Massachusetts, 2012.

———. *The Papers of Francis Bernard: Governor of Colonial Massachusetts, 1760–69, Vol. 4: 1768.* Vol. 86. Boston: Colonial Society of Massachusetts, 2015.

Novanglus, And Massachusettensis; Or, Political Essays, Published in the Years 1774 And 1775. Boston: Printed and published by Hews & Goss, 1819.

O'Callaghan, E. B., ed. *Documents relative to the colonial history of the State of New-York; procured in Holland, England, and France.* Vol. 7. Albany: New York State Legislature, 1856.

Otis, James. *The Rights of the British Colonies Asserted and Proved.* Boston, 1764.

The Parliamentary History of England, From the Earliest Period to the Year 1803. Vol. 15, A.D. 1753–1765. London: Printed by T.C. Hansard, 1813.

———. Vol. 16, A.D. 1765–1771. London: Printed by T.C. Hansard, 1813.

———. Vol. 17, A.D. 1771–1774. London: Printed by T.C. Hansard, 1813.

Pickering, Danby. *Statutes at Large*. Vol. 16. Cambridge, UK: Printed by Joseph Bentham, 1765.

Pitman, Frank Wesley. *The Development of the British West Indies, 1700–1763*. New Haven, CT: Archon Books, 1917.

Price, Richard. *Observations on the Nature of Civil Liberty, the Principles of Government, and the Justice and Policy of the War with America*. London: Printed for T. Cadell, 1776.

Publications of the Colonial Society of Massachusetts. Vol. 19, *Transactions, 1916–1917*. Boston, 1918.

The Public Records of the Colony of Connecticut [1636–1776]. Vol. 9. Hartford, CT: Press of the Case, 1890.

Reid, John Philip. *The Authority to Tax*. Vol. 2 of *Constitutional History of the American Revolution*. Madison: University of Wisconsin Press, 1987.

A Report of the Record Commissioners of the City of Boston Containing the Boston Town Records, 1758–1769. Boston: Rockwell and Churchill, 1886.

Ricord, Frederick W., and Wm. Nelson, eds. *Documents Relating to the Colonial History of the State of New Jersey*. Vol. 9. Newark: New Jersey Historical Society, 1885.

Saunders, William L., ed. *The Colonial Records of North Carolina*. Vol. 6. Raleigh: Joseph Daniels, 1888.

Shy, John. *Toward Lexington: The Role of the British Army in the Coming of the American Revolution*. Princeton, NJ: Princeton University Press, 1965.

Simmons, R. C., and P. D. G. Thomas, eds. *Proceedings and debates of the British Parliaments respecting North America, 1754–1783*. Vol. 1, *1754-1764*. Millwood, NY: Kraus International, 1982.

Smith, William James, ed. *The Grenville papers: being the correspondence of Richard Grenville, earl Temple, K.G., and the right Hon. George Grenville, their friends and contemporaries*. Vol. 2. London: John Murray, 1852.

Tenth Report of the Royal Commission on Historical Manuscripts. London: H. M. Stationery Office, 1885.

Thomas, P. D. G. *The House of Commons in the Eighteenth Century*. Oxford: Clarendon Press, 1971.

———. *British Politics and the Stamp Act Crisis: The First Phase of the American Revolution, 1763–1767.* Oxford: Clarendon Press, 1975.

———. *Revolution in America: Britain and the Colonies, 1763–1776.* Cardiff: University of Wales Press, 1992.

Tyler, John W., and Elizabeth Dubrulle, eds. *The Correspondence of Thomas Hutchinson, Vol. 1, 1740–1766.* Vol. 84. Boston: Colonial Society of Massachusetts, 2014.

Whately, Thomas. *The Regulations Lately Made Concerning the Colonies, and the Taxes Imposed Upon Them, Considered.* London: Printed for J. Wilkie, 1765.

Wood, Gordon S. *The Creation of the American Republic, 1776–1787.* Chapel Hill: University of North Carolina Press, 1969.

———, ed. *The American Revolution: Writings from the Pamphlet Debate 1764–1776.* Vol. 1. New York: Library of America, 2015.

Articles

Barrow, Thomas C. "Background to the Grenville Program, 1757–1763." *William and Mary Quarterly* 22, no. 1 (1965): 93-104.

———. "A Project for Imperial Reform." *William and Mary Quarterly* 24, no. 1 (1967): 108-26.

Johnson, Allen S. "The Passage of the Sugar Act." *William and Mary Quarterly* 16, no. 4 (1959): 507-14.

"Journal, December 1764: Vol. 71." *Journals of the Board of Trade and Plantations, Vol. 12, January 1764–December 1767.* Edited by K. H. Ledward (1936): 120-31. *British History Online.* Accessed October 5, 2020. http://www.british-history.ac.uk/jrnl-trade-plantations/vol12/pp120-131.

Miller, E. J. "The Virginia Legislature and the Stamp Act." *William and Mary Quarterly* 21, no. 4 (1913): 233-48.

Morgan, Edmund S. "Colonial Ideas of Parliamentary Power 1764–1766." *William and Mary Quarterly* 5, no. 3 (1948): 311-41.

———, "The Postponement of the Stamp Act." *William and Mary Quarterly* 7, no. 3 (1950): 353-92.

Namier, L. B. "Charles Garth, Agent for South Carolina: Part 2 (Continued)." *English Historical Review* 54, no. 216 (1939): 632-52.

Shumate, Ken. "The Molasses Act: A Brief History." *Journal of the American Revolution: Annual Volume 2020*. Vol. 8 (2020): 8-20.

———. "Reasons Against the Renewal of the Sugar Act." *Journal of the American Revolution*, June 4, 11, and 18, 2020.

———. "The Sugar Act: A Brief History." *Journal of the American Revolution*, September 17, 2018.

Southwick, Albert B. "The Molasses Act—Source of Precedents." *William and Mary Quarterly* 8, no. 3 (1951): 389-405.

Taylor, Robert J. "Israel Mauduit." *New England Quarterly* 24, no. 2 (1951): 208-30.

Thomas, P. D. G., ed. "Parliamentary Diaries of Nathaniel Ryder, 1764–7." *Camden Miscellany* 23, 4th ser., vol. 7 (1969): 256-57.

Virginia Historical Society. "Proceedings of the Virginia Committee of Correspondence, 1759–1767." *Virginia Magazine of History and Biography* 12, no. 1 (1904): 1-14.

———. "Virginia Legislative Documents." *Virginia Magazine of History and Biography* 9, no. 4 (1902): 353-68.

———. "Virginia Legislative Documents (continued)." *Virginia Magazine of History and Biography* 10, no. 1 (1902): 1-16.

Wiener, Frederick Bernays. "The Rhode Island Merchants and the Sugar Act." *New England Quarterly* 3, no. 3 (1930): 464-500.

INDEX